ROOTED IN L

CISTERCIAN STUDIES SERIES: NUMBER TWO-HUNDRED SEVENTEEN

ROOTED IN DETACHMENT

Living the Transfiguration

KENNETH STEVENSON

Cistercian Publications
Kalamazoo, Michigan

First published in 2007 by
Darton, Longman and Todd Ltd
1 Spencer Court
140–142 Wandsworth High Street
London SW18 4JJ

First published in the USA by
Cistercian Publications
Institute of Cistercian Studies
WMU Station
Kalamazoo, Michigan 49008-5415
http://www.cistercianpublications.org

Customer service:
Liturgical Press
Collegeville, Minnesota 56321-7500
Tel: 1-800-436-8431
E-mail: sales@litpress.org

ISBN 978-0-87907-517-0

Phototypeset by YHT Ltd, London
Printed and bound in Great Britain

CONTENTS

PREFACE

It's something of a surprise that the Transfiguration of Christ – described in three gospels and the Second Letter of Peter – has received so little attention in recent times. New Testament scholars continue to probe into its origins and significance, and in that connection, my debt to the work of John Paul Heil (2000) and Dorothy Lee (2004) is obvious. But so far there have been scarcely any books on its place in the tradition of interpretation, Western as well as Eastern, with the exception of John Anthony McGuckin's study of the patristic period (1986). A crucial issue in the tradition is the apparent conflict between reading the narrative in connection with Lent ('glory before cross') and the Feast on 6 August, which is a later development. Many years ago, Michael Ramsey (1949) wrote a biblically based work which embraced theological and liturgical considerations as well. What follows has been inspired by that seminal book – down to the title, 'rooted in detachment', one of Ramsey's pithy and perceptive ways of describing the Transfiguration.

This book really began a long time ago. My parents, Erik and Margrethe Stevenson, taught me to think about the Transfiguration as a teenager, and when my mother died in the autumn of 2004, a copy of *The Cloud of Unknowing*, one of her favourites, was placed on her coffin for the funeral. By this time, I had already decided to write on the three gospel narratives from the perspective of how they have been interpreted down the ages, and to do so with the help of

Eastern iconography. Another dimension broke in on my life, when I was diagnosed with acute myeloid leukaemia early in September the year before last. My experience of the ensuing treatment, in the Haematology Unit of the Queen Alexandra Hospital, Portsmouth, and subsequently for a bone marrow transplant at the Southampton General Hospital, has left a lasting mark on me, and I am profoundly grateful to the doctors, nurses, chaplains, and support staff for their care for me as I slowly responded to what was the greatest challenge I had so far faced in my life. What they did for me, and the prayers of many people, lies behind the pages that follow.

Time, always a precious commodity, was at a premium: all the way through the courses of chemotherapy, the subsequent infections, and the aftermaths at home, I was able to soak myself in the authors investigated here, and many others as well. A pattern began to emerge in my mind for each chapter: an introduction, based around the icon of Theophanes the Greek; a consideration of the gospel narratives in all their variations; one major writer's 'take' on the Transfiguration, with an emphasis on the episode in question; followed by a devotional conclusion. I have tried to make the selection of authors as comprehensive as possible, but in confining myself to those who have written specifically on the Transfiguration, some obvious twentieth-century authors (like Von Balthasar and Rahner) have not made it in the end – sorry! This is, however, a book by a Westerner, offered in the spirit of friendship with the East, where the Transfiguration has long held a more central place.

Many people deserve my thanks, over and above the hospital staff I have just mentioned. Brendan Walsh gave the original invitation to write; Quarr Abbey, as always, provided an atmosphere of prayer and a well-stocked library in the earlier stages, since when Brother Duncan has been unfailingly helpful in answering cries for help from sickbed or convalescence; the same is true of Harald Buchinger in Rome, Simon Jones in Oxford and Brian Streeter in Cambridge;

Jeremy Ames helped over icons; Michael Bury with Raphael's 'Transfiguration'; Christian Thodberg helped me yet again with Grundtvig, the enigmatic Dane; Calum Macfarlane put me onto John Hacket, the most prolific preacher on the subject; Andrew Louth assisted me over Maximus, and the later East; Geoffrey Rowell and Rowan Williams steered me at important stages; Bob Taft gave me much encouragement through the illness, as did John and Lydia Gladwin and Martin Kitchen, with their regular phone calls, Martin also providing wisdom on New Testament issues. My colleagues, Michael Jordan, Chris Lowson (before his move), Peter Hancock, Trevor Reader, Caroline Baston, Wendy Kennedy and Alex Hughes kept the diocesan show on the road, with episcopal assistance from Trevor Wilmott; and Alex also gently managed the household here, Michael Chipperfield, Jean Maslin, Julie Anderson, Judy Couzens and Jenny Swatton; then there is always my family, Sarah and our children, Elisabeth, Kitty – who read the draft in full and made many wise comments – (and David), James (and Nicky), newly-born grandson Jacob, and Alexandra, all of whose love and presence were essential for this book to be brought to birth.

To all these people, and the many others who prayed for me through my illness, this book is dedicated with deep gratitude.

Kenneth Stevenson　　　　　　　　　　　　Easter 2007
Bishopsgrove
Fareham

THE TRANSFIGURATION NARRATIVES

MARK	MATTHEW	LUKE
'Truly I tell you, there are some standing here who will not taste death until they see *that the Kingdom of God has come with power*.' (Mark 9:1)	'Truly I tell you, there are some standing here who will not taste death before they see *the Son of Man coming in his Kingdom*.' (Matt. 16:28)	'But truly I tell you, there are some standing here who will not taste death before they see *the Kingdom of God*.' (Luke 9:27)
Six days later, Jesus took with him Peter and James and John, and led them up a high mountain *apart*, by themselves. (Mark 9:2)	Six days later, Jesus took with him Peter and James and *his brother* John and led them up a high mountain, by themselves. (Matt. 17:1)	*Now about eight days after these sayings*, Jesus took with him Peter and John and James, and *went up on the mountain to pray*. (Luke 9:28)
And he was transfigured before them, and his clothes became dazzling white, *such as no one on earth could bleach them*. (Mark 9:3)	And he was transfigured before them, and his face *shone like the sun*, and his clothes became dazzling white. (Matt. 17:2)	And *while he was praying, the appearance of his face changed*, and his clothes became dazzling white. (Luke 9:29)
And there appeared to them *Elijah with Moses*, who were talking with Jesus. (Mark 9:4)	Suddenly there appeared to them Moses and Elijah talking to him. (Matt. 17:3)	Suddenly *they saw two men*, Moses and Elijah, talking to him. *They appeared in glory and were speaking of his departure, which he was about to accomplish at Jerusalem. Now Peter and his companions were weighed down with sleep, but since they had stayed awake, they saw his glory and the two men who stood with him.'* (Luke 9:30–32)

Mark	Matthew	Luke
Then Peter said to Jesus, *'Rabbi,* it is good for us to be here; let us make three dwellings, one for you, one for Moses, and one for Elijah.' *He did not know what to say, for they were terrified.* (Mark 9:5–6)	Then Peter said to Jesus, *'Lord,* it is good for us to be here; *if you wish, I will* make three dwellings here, one for you, one for Moses, and one for Elijah.' (Matt. 17:4)	*Just as they were leaving him,* Peter said to Jesus, *'Master,* it is good for us to be here; let us make three dwellings, one for you, one for Moses, and one for Elijah' – *not knowing what he said.* (Luke 9:33)
Then a cloud overshadowed them. (Mark 9:7a)	*While he was still speaking, suddenly a bright* cloud overshadowed them. (Matt. 17:5a)	*While he was saying this,* a cloud overshadowed them, *and they were terrified as they entered the cloud.* (Luke 9:34)
'And from the cloud there came a voice, "This is my Son, the Beloved, listen to him!" *Suddenly when they* looked around, they saw no one *with them any more, but only Jesus.'* (Mark 9:7b–8)	And from the cloud a voice said, *'This is my Son, the Beloved, with him I am well pleased;* listen to him!' *When the disciples heard this they fell to the ground and were overcome by fear. But Jesus came and touched them, saying, 'Get up and do not be afraid.' And when they looked up, they saw no-one except Jesus himself alone.* (Matt. 17:5b–8)	*Then* from the cloud came a voice *that* said, 'This is my Son, *my Chosen,* listen to him!' *When the voice had spoken, Jesus* was found alone. (Luke 9:35–36a)
As they were coming down the mountain, *he* ordered them *to* tell no one about what they had seen, until after the Son of Man had *risen* from the dead. (Mark 8:9)	As they were coming down the mountain, *Jesus* ordered them, "Tell no one *about the vision* until after the Son of Man has *been raised* from the dead.' (Matt. 17:9)	*And they kept silent and in those days told no one any of the things they had seen.* (Luke 9:36b)
MARK	**MATTHEW**	**LUKE**

Chapter 1

ICON AS NARRATIVE

The Transfiguration stands as a gateway to the saving events of the Gospel.

(A. M. Ramsey, 1904–88)[1]

In the Tretyakov Gallery in Moscow there is an icon of the Transfiguration. As one looks at it, the eye is taken straight to the central figure of Christ, bathed in white, with the two figures of Moses and Elijah on either side in deep yellow and brown. Below are the three disciples, Peter, James and John, also in yellow and brown, terror-struck by what is going on above them. But they are not cut off from the action, because each of them is at the receiving end of a blue ray emanating from Christ. There is also one detail not unknown in later Transfiguration icons that does not appear in earlier ones. Between the three upper figures and the three lower figures, as if both to exaggerate and to minimise the distance between the two zones, there are two much smaller scenes, which depict Jesus and the disciples ascending the mountain and then descending it. And as if to make the point that this is all about Christ himself, he stands out as the leader. He leads them up the mountain but he also leads them down.

Icons are impossible to put into words, and this particular

1

example, painted by Theophanes the Greek around the year 1403, is no exception. If I could describe it, there would be no point in painting (or 'writing' as it's technically called) in the first place. Unlike many in the earlier Greek style, this icon has no golden background that swoops all the figures into eternity and brings them right under our very noses. Instead the perspectives on eternity and history are shown primarily by the gold-backed Christ-figure, gleaming in white, and drawing both past (Moses and Elijah) and present (the three disciples) into a new kind of understanding of who they are and what they are called to be and do. In his study of the relationship between Byzantine Transfiguration iconography and theology, Andreas Andreopoulos shows how central this particular tradition has been and continues to be; indeed it is the scene that trainee icon-painters traditionally cut their teeth on; and the tradition for this scene is remarkable enough in itself.[2] That suggests a kind of confirmation of what Michael Ramsey writes towards the end of his little masterpiece, *The Glory of God and the Transfiguration of Christ*, probably the only great book written on this subject in the twentieth century: 'The Transfiguration stands as a gateway to the saving events of the Gospel.'

The trouble with the word 'icon' is that it has come to be used in so many connections in recent years. In some ways, this is a reversion to its original meaning: icon is, quite simply, the Greek word for a picture. And only four centuries ago, when the English language imported Greek and Latin words, all it meant was a likeness, whether in the form of a statue or, later on, an illustration in a book. It was only in the 1830s, when interest in the Christian East began to be felt, that 'icon' took on a new lease of life: an icon became a holy picture, painted according to established rules in the Greek or Russian manner, with stylised figures, haloes on their heads, and (usually) confined to certain set scenes in the life of Christ or the saints. The load which the word began to bear was religious, and the figures always special. All this means that the

2

difficulties in using the word more widely today are compounded by the fact that the secular icon is neither Christ, nor one of his followers in whom his redeeming grace has begun to triumph. Instead, it is a celebrity, someone held up to be ideal, someone glamorous, likeable, perhaps, but all the time waiting for the newspaper coverage of something shady from the past, or else a piece of bad luck in the future.

There is nothing that has to be of necessity wrong or evil in the culture in which we are set. What Christians are called to do is identify its weaknesses, which we share with our contemporaries, as well celebrate and extend its strengths and challenges: the prophetic spirit can just as easily speak from right outside the confines of the community of faith, as both the Old and New Testaments make clear. That word 'transfigure' is a case in point, the 'Christianisation' of a word with a pagan background. It is taken from a Latin word, *transfiguro*, used around the time of Christ by writers such as Ovid (43 BC– c. AD 17), to describe the 'changes in form' of gods and people in his (mainly Greek) stories, called the *Metamorphoses*, the long-established Greek word for the process. 'Transfigure' was therefore the obvious word to use when translating how Jesus was 'metamorphosed' on the mountain, as the Greek original puts it in two of the gospel narratives (Matt. 17:2; Mark 9:2). St Paul uses exactly the same word, 'metamorphose', 'change in form', when describing how the Christian is to be transformed into the image of Christ (2 Cor. 3:18), a transformation and renewal that starts in this life by our not being conformed to this world (Rom. 12:2). Here is a prime example of a word being 'baptised' by Christianity. The first known early Latin Christian writer to use *transfiguro* was Tertullian (*c.* 160–*c.* 225) in North Africa, echoing the version of the Latin Bible he used. The term as used in the New Testament, whether in the gospels or by Paul in his letters, is about a profound change, by God in the Christ through the Spirit. Transfiguration therefore is not like a picture of something long dead and gone but resembles more an icon

3

that draws us into its own narrative, which is the life of God among us now.

The icon by Theophanes, unlike many others, includes those smaller scenes of the trudge up the mountain and the walk back down. In other words, there is both ascent and descent. In order to see the transfigured Christ, we have to leave behind the familiar, but we also have to come down again; there can be no staying permanently in an unnaturally extended religious comfort zone. Interestingly, the painter of that icon takes care to depict Christ paying even more attention to the disciples on the way down than on the way up! But there is another reason for the choice: it is because of the Russian way of mixing the heavenly and the earthly, the white and shining Christ-figure surrounded by landscape and humanity in dirty yellows and browns. And just to make the point of the relationship between eternity and history even more subtle, it is in the *hands* of the figures that the challenges are perhaps most expressed, whether it is the welcoming Christ, the quizzical Moses and Elijah, or the terror-struck yearning of Peter, James and John. Here we do not see celebrities, in all their glossy and superficial perfection, tottering on their fragile way. Instead we see ourselves and our own world judged, challenged, and beautified – *and* faced down as well.

The Theophanes icon, therefore, is a narrative of the Transfiguration. It is no static scene, but is full of movement, telling the events recorded in the first three gospels (Mark 9:1–9; Matt. 16:28—17:9; Luke 9:27–37) as well as (more briefly) right at the end of the New Testament (2 Pet. 1:16–19). To see the icon as a narrative is to open one's eyes to a different, more allusive way of looking at the gospel than many of us do most of the time. We are not just dealing with words, nor with comparing and contrasting the different ways in which the gospel-writers work (important though that is). We are dealing with events, with human beings, and the way Jesus confronts those events – Israel's past – and challenges and renews his own followers as well. But the icon cannot tell the whole

4

story. The icon is there to help us to pray. And that is one of the reasons why it has to direct us to the biblical narratives that inspired the iconographer in the first place. To these we shall now briefly turn, as an introduction to the more detailed reflections that will come later on with each of the succeeding chapters, whose themes are promise, ascent, change, visitors, enthusiasm, cloud, voice and descent.

While New Testament commentaries on the gospels of Matthew, Mark and Luke all discuss the Transfiguration from their respective points of view,[3] there have been very few books specifically on this subject. Two recent studies are notable exceptions. John Paul Heil looks at the narratives from the point of view of their relationship with the rest of each gospel.[4] Dorothy Lee, on the other hand, examines each narrative, comparing them with each other, but with the rest of the New Testament as well.[5] While New Testament scholars in the past have concentrated on what they thought lies behind the gospel narratives, a refreshing development in recent years, reflected partly in Lee's book, is attention to the way the narratives have been interpreted down the centuries, the 'reception-history' of the gospels.[6] Here is a prime example of the importance of not seeing biblical studies living in a separate world from historical theology, and in that connection we must not overlook John McGuckin's ground-breaking comparative study of the Transfiguration in the Greek and Latin Fathers of the first millennium.[7] Because of the richness of the traditions associated with the Transfiguration, it is something of a surprise that these treasures, one of the main features of the pages that follow, have not been opened up more fully before. Regardless of what was included in the narratives and what was not, they have still been read by different groups of people, in some very different contexts, whether as part of Lenten (or pre-Lenten) discipline, as a special festival on 6 August, or on some other occasion, perhaps as the topic of a special sermon or series of sermons.

What, then, of the narratives themselves, in the context of the gospel-writers? Today's consensus – although not entirely unanimous – is that Mark's gospel is the earliest of the three. It is the shortest, and its portrait of Jesus is by far the most enigmatic. All the time, the underlying question concerns Jesus' identity, and the extent to which this is either revealed by Jesus (does he know it himself?), or understood by his followers. As Lee puts it: 'The theme of the [Marcan narrative] is primarily Jesus' identity, which is both manifest and secret at the same time.'[8] This is shown in the three main variants in the Transfiguration narrative. The first is that, unlike Matthew and Luke, there is no reference to Jesus' face (Mark 9:2); the second is the almost wistful reference to Jesus' dazzling garments, 'such that no one on earth could bleach' (Mark 9:2), pointing to the heavenly character of the transforming clothing; and the third is when Peter is depicted as not knowing what to say when he suggests building three tabernacles (Mark 9:6). Mark's overall style is simple, sharp-edged, and as enigmatic as Jesus himself. And, as we shall see, it is his gospel which uses the 'inner cabinet' of Peter, James and John more than the others, and which highlights their lack of understanding, *even* after the revelation on the mountain; in the middle of the very next chapter James and John themselves ask for ringside seats in the Kingdom (Mark 10:35).

Mark's narrative is both simple and unique. But hardly any sermons specifically on his version have come down to us. Jerome, good biblical scholar that he was, preached on it, probably at some time between 394 and 413. And he shows no signs of a tendency we shall come across in other preachers to harmonise the gospel-variants, instead pointing up the three special features we have just identified (ch. 2). Bishop John Wordsworth (1843–1911), on the other hand, preaching what turned out to be his very last sermon, to the students of Salisbury Theological College, on 6 August 1911, uses the opening words of Mark's narrative as the text (Mark 9:2), but then goes on to suggest that Luke's narrative should be used in any officially authorised Anglican revision![9] The Venerable Bede's commentaries on the three gospel narratives, on the other hand, which come from Northumbria in the first part of the eighth century, show a profound awareness of their variants.[10]

With Matthew's gospel, we are by contrast faced with the most read narrative of all, because of the position given to Matthew as the 'first gospel' from earliest times. Both Mark and Matthew refer to 'a high mountain' (Mark 9:2; Matt. 17:1), but for Matthew mountains are very significant. It is from 'the mountain' that Jesus delivers the Sermon on the Mount (Matt. 5:1); it is to 'the mountain' that Jesus goes to pray (Matt. 14:23); and it is on 'the mountain' that Jesus heals the sick who are brought to him (Matt. 15:29). And, after the mountain of Transfiguration, there follows death and resurrection, leading on to the final mountain, where Jesus commissions the disciples to go out and proclaim his message (Matt. 28:19–20). Matthew, the most Jewish of the gospel-writers, sees Jesus as the heir of Moses, with the new Law, which is about the new Kingdom, proclaimed in the Beatitudes on that mountain, the heavenly Kingdom which is echoed in the opening words of the Lord's Prayer (Matt. 6:9–13). If Graham Stanton is right, the community that produced this gospel were thrown out of the synagogue and were forced to claim their identity in the proclaimed Jesus who had superseded Moses.[11] This means that the variants in his narrative are crucial. Jesus' face is mentioned, shining like the sun (Matt. 17:2), in order to compare him with Moses on Mount Sinai (Exod. 34:29–35). He reverses the order of Elijah and Moses from Mark's account (Matt. 17:3; cf. Mark 9:4). The Voice adds the words 'in whom I am well pleased' (Matt. 17:5), in order to underline his uniqueness, and to refer back to Jesus' baptism (Matt. 3:17). And the awesome evocation of the memory of Sinai is redoubled with Matthew's important addition at the end, when the disciples are full of fear, and Jesus comes to them, touches them, and tells them to rise up and not be afraid (Matt. 17:6–8), thus complementing the Voice that has spoken. Here is the new Moses indeed! As Lee puts it, 'On the mount of transfiguration, [Jesus] re-enacts the story of Moses' ascent up Mount Sinai, revealing himself as the one who embodies the law in word and deed.'[12]

We shall be encountering more treatment of Matthew's narrative than any other, for the simple reason that until the liturgical changes of recent years, his was the gospel passage that was usually read in the West. This is still the case for the Eucharist on 6 August in much of the East. There are a number of consequences, principally the sheer stability of knowing one version, and one only, as well as the observable fact that iconography, for example, tends to reflect Matthew's features, if any at all. The icon described earlier makes much of the disciples' fear, with Christ almost appearing as if he is about to go down to them, touch them, and tell them to rise up and not be afraid. All this comes across in the many expositions and sermons of the Matthew account that we shall be looking at, whether by John Chrysostom (*c.* 347–407) in late fourth-century Antioch (see Chapter 5) or Nikolai Grundtvig (1783–1872) in mid nineteenth-century Copenhagen (see Chapter 4). To the contemporary informed reader, accustomed to enjoying all three narratives in turn, such a concentration on Matthew may come across as lopsided, but it is still the principal choice of tradition, whether we like it or not.

When it comes to Luke's gospel, we are on different territory altogether. Here is Jesus as the Lord of history, the middle of time, to echo the original German title of Hans Conzelmann's study some years ago.[13] The portrait is still somewhat impressionistic, but there is always a greater sense of history unfolding than in either of the other gospels; hence, for example, the care with which Jesus' birth is set in the much wider context of Roman Emperor and Roman governor (Luke 2:1), to say nothing of the list of ruling worthies that head up the following chapter, at the start of Jesus' public ministry (Luke 3:1). With Luke, of course, we have the added advantage of two books, the gospel of Jesus and a history of the early church: hence the way that the former ends and the latter begins with the ascension, the culmination of Christ's life and ministry (Luke 24:44–53; Acts 1:6–11). The variants in his narrative underscore these concerns. 'After about eight days' (Luke 9:28) more obviously symbolises completion than 'after six days' in the other two accounts (Matt. 17:1; Mark 9:2). Then, Jesus goes up to the mountain to *pray* (Luke 9:28), as he does at other significant points in his ministry, demonstrating his close relationship with the Father: at his baptism (Luke 3:21), before calling the disciples (Luke 6:12), before asking them about his identity (Luke 9:18), as well as in Gethsemane (Luke 22:40f), to say nothing of the poignant moment when he prays for those who are crucifying him (Luke 23:34). And then we have the special feature which, along with Jesus praying, is picked up by numerous preachers, even though they are basing themselves on Matthew(!), namely the way Moses and Elijah discuss with Jesus his *exodus* ('departure') at Jerusalem. Luke, the historian gospel-writer, binds into his account a sense of purpose, prayer, and a direct relationship between this particular episode and those which follow.

As we have just pointed out, Luke is referred to by Matthew-inspired preachers, just as not a few pick up the fact that Mark asserts that no earthly bleacher could provide a whiter garment (Mark 9:3). But unlike Mark, who attracts barely any daring expositor of old, there is a steady trickle of Luke-orientated writing, for example the commentary by Ambrose of Milan (*c.* 339–97), and the sermons by Cyril of Alexandria (d. 444), Proclus of Constantinople (d. 446), followed by Timothy of Jerusalem in the sixth century, who is the most particular of the three in using the Lucan variants.[14] Much later on, Luke acquires a special place among Anglican preachers. We noted earlier John Wordsworth championing him. In the seventeenth century, as we shall see, both John

Hacket (1590–1670; see Chapter 3) and Mark Frank (1613–64) based their preaching on his narrative (see Chapter 6), in Hacket's case providing us with the most extensive course of sermons on the Transfiguration so far known. It is not hard to find an explanation, which may well be a mixture of the need to move away from Matthew's prominence, as well as sheer entrancement with Luke's unique features. It may also have something to do with another of Luke's variants, the way he resists using the word 'transfigured' for the more impressionistic 'change in the appearance' of Jesus' face (Luke 9:29).

So far, we have concentrated on the gospel accounts, which inevitably leads to some consideration of how all this fits in with the liturgical tradition, how these narratives have been 'read' across the centuries. Indeed, one of the strengths of Heil's study is that he places the 'reader' (for him, the 'audience') as the challenged participant in each gospel from the very beginning, so that the Transfiguration, while being still a profound surprise, 'pivots the audience back' to understand its meaning both in the light of Jesus' teaching about suffering and about the events about to unfold in relation to our redemption. As he puts it, 'heavenly glory lies not in the wish to escape but in the courage to embrace rejection, suffering, and death.'[15] It is this holistic insight on the Transfiguration, as an integral part of each gospel, that is an important marker to put down now, before we embark on how it has been interpreted down the ages.

But we need to look briefly at the way transfiguration fares in the rest of the New Testament. There is no Transfiguration narrative in the Fourth Gospel, because it is shot through with 'transfiguration' from start to finish. 'After three days', the only time indication in the entire gospel and one that expresses completion in another way, Jesus performs the first of his great 'signs', at the wedding in Cana (John 2:1–11). Michael Ramsey[16] makes a great deal of this theme, echoed in the root meaning of glory as 'reputation', 'renown', signalled at the very start, with the 'glory' of the incarnate Word (John

10

1:14), and continuing with the other signs: the healing of the nobleman's son (John 4:46–54), the impotent man (John 5:2–9), the feeding of the five thousand (John 6:4–13), the healing of the man born blind (John 9:1–7), and the raising of Lazarus from the dead (John 11:1–44). And he pushes the theme further into the Upper Room, with transformation dominating the mood of the so-called Farewell Discourses (John 13—16) and the 'High Priestly Prayer' where Jesus offers himself to the Father (John 17) in a way that suggests that glory and cross are so closely linked as to be indistinguishable from each other. In the sermons and expositions of the Transfiguration we shall be looking at, the Fourth Gospel is sometimes in the background, for example in the rich preaching in the fourteenth century of Gregory Palamas (c. 1296–1359; see Chapter 7), where John seems to provide something of a 'frame' for what he has to say.

The same is true, to a lesser extent, of 'transforming' texts in St Paul, whether of seeing Christ with unveiled face (2 Cor. 3:16–18), Christ's humility and exaltation (Phil. 2:5–11), or of our bodies being transformed (Phil. 3:21).[17] But the most used text by far is the testimony of the author of the Second Letter of Peter (2 Pet. 1:16–19), where apostolic witness is central, but with a shortened narrative that mentions the mountain, the changed appearance of Jesus, and the voice, but not Moses and Elijah, Peter's response, or the fear of the disciples, or the cloud.[18] This is the passage most frequently adopted for the epistle reading for the Transfiguration as a feast in its own right, rather than as a narrative read in connection with Lenten observance, and understandably so.

Space precludes a proper treatment of the rest of the New Testament, since our concern is with the tradition of interpretation of the narratives themselves. For the icon of the Transfiguration is invariably inspired by the three gospel narratives, even if it has tended to concentrate on Matthew's version more than the other two. Central to the Transfiguration's position in all three gospels is its relationship to the cross, in Matthew and Mark, but a few chapters further on (Matt. 26—27; Mark 14—15), whereas in Luke there is much more of a gap (Luke 22—23), perhaps in part compensated for by Luke's insertion of the reference to Moses and Elijah talking about just this, the 'departure at Jerusalem' (Luke 9:31). Indeed, Jesus has already predicted his impending death beforehand (Matt. 16:21ff; Mark 8:31ff; Luke 9:21ff), with Peter refusing to accept it, and no sooner have the four of them come down from the mountain than Jesus begins to take up the same theme (Matt. 17:9ff; Mark 9:9ff, Luke 9:44f).

How, then, do the icon and the living gospel narrative transfer into worship, whether in the collective context of a liturgy, or the simple use of a prayer-card in a Bible on which an icon may be illustrated? The answer is that the 'transference' has already begun. We need to break down these neat distinctions. You cannot have icon without gospel narrative, and gospel narrative inevitably forms some sort of scene in the mind. The Transfiguration is so vivid and central a scene that it has audience participation from the word go, which 'pivots' back into the rest of the gospel. In that sense, it is indeed a 'gateway' to the cross, and beyond. And that is why the Christian tradition has never quite known how to handle it.

In the Christian West, contemporary use of the Transfiguration narrative in the liturgy is lavish, which is why it is all the more important to think more deeply about it. It is read before or near the start of Lent, in order to relate it directly with those central events of Christ's death and resurrection which it is supposed to prefigure, not as a kind of pre-packaged reward in advance, in order to soften the pain, but as both a hope and a warning that the two belong together. The Roman Catholic Lectionary of 1969 stays with the Second Sunday in Lent, where it has been read since 1474, the difference being that the three gospels are read in sequence each year. But the earlier practice was not to read it on the Sunday, but from at least the time of Pope Leo the Great (d. 460) it was the Gospel set for the 'Ember' Saturday, the day before, when ordinations took place, though, in the context of a Vigil Mass, in practice the Gospel was (at least originally), read early on the Sunday morning. John Chrysostom preached a course of sermons on Matthew's gospel while a presbyter in Antioch in 390, among which was an exposition of the Transfiguration generally thought to have been delivered in Lent (see Chapter 5).[19] This older tradition, which has nothing to do with a festival at all, will keep recurring among the preachers and expositors we shall be looking at. Modern ecumenical take-up of the Roman lectionary, Anglican and Lutheran included, tends to make a significant adaptation, by reading the Transfiguration narrative on the Sunday before Lent, so that it becomes a kind of 'bookend' to the start of the solemn season; this may be partly because at the time of the Reformation northern Europe had not caught up with the change made for the Second Sunday in Lent in Rome in 1474.

What, then, of the 6 August festival? Evidence suggests that it began in and around Jerusalem in the fourth and fifth centuries, and the day was chosen in order to be exactly forty days before 14 September, Holy Cross Day, because of a tradition that the Transfiguration took place forty days before the crucifixion.[20] Jerusalem included in its ecclesiastical jurisdiction St Catherine's Monastery on Mount Sinai, with its magnificent mosaic of the Transfiguration dating from the mid sixth century, which Andreopoulos has shown is central to the development of subsequent iconography.[21] The feast probably reached Constantinople during the time of the great hymn-writer Andrew of Crete (c. 660–740), who was a monk at the Church of the Holy Sepulchre from 675 until 685, when he moved to serve at the Great Church of Sancta Sophia, Constantinople, after which he became Archbishop of Gortyna in Crete. It was a major feast, which developed a magnificent series of hymns and lections,

ating for Matthew's version at the Eucharist with Mattins.

One of the main motivations for the shift in the Orthodox East from exposition of the narrative to introducing the feast seems to have been its christological importance – about both the humanity and the divinity of Christ manifested to the disciples and (by extension) to us. The subsequent trade route sees it slowly appearing in the West, but as a minor feast only, at first in Spain in the eleventh century. This was followed in a magnificent push by Peter the Venerable (1092/1094–1156), Abbot of Cluny from 1122 to 1156 (see Chapter 8), who directed its observance in all Cluniac communities in 1132.[22] Already established in different ways in different parts of the Catholic world, it was officially imposed in 1457 by Pope Callixtus III, a Valencian sensitive to the memory of Moorish domination in Spain, who used as a pretext the Christian defeat of the Turks at Belgrade on 22 July in the previous year, news of which had reached Rome on 6 August – it was a world far removed from today's inter-faith conversations and collaboration in community-building. Biblical as the feast was in origin, it was too recent an addition to impress the Reformers. It disappeared from view in the 1549 English Prayer Book, although it reappeared in 1662, but in the calendar only, lying somewhat dormant until its revival in the nineteenth century.

We are thus faced with what is in origin an Eastern festival, inspired by associations with Mount Tabor, a hill to the south-west of the Sea of Galilee under two thousand feet high. Somehow it has reached the Christian West, but without the central place it occupies in the Orthodox Calendar as one of the Twelve Feasts, though even here Andreopoulos has doubts about its appropriateness in August, when it is over-shadowed by the Dormition (Assumption) on 15 August; he, too, thinks it belongs in Lent.[23] But there are other uses, too, which we shall encounter. At the Danish Lutheran Reforma-tion, the Transfiguration narrative was thought too good

14

entirely to lose; hence its appearance from 1556 onwards, tucked away at the very back of beyond in the Church's year – the 27th Sunday after Trinity or the 6th after Epiphany. These were occasions for which medieval books made no provision, probably because they only occurred every so often, due the vagaries of the Church's year. We shall be looking at Grundtvig's preaching and hymnody for these Sundays (see Chapter 4). Then there is an altogether novel approach, probably adopted by other preachers down the ages, which is to preach a course of sermons on the narrative at a convenient time somewhere else in the year; a prime example is John Hacket, in seventeenth-century London, for whom the Transfiguration belongs firmly in the season of Easter (see Chapter 4). As each chapter unfolds, with its treatment of the gospel narratives for each episode, and its coverage of specific authors chosen for their way of handling the event, the Transfiguration will emerge in an ever richer light.

History does not 'solve' the Transfiguration, because it is too rich and complex to belong in any one corner. Today's exposure to all three gospel-writers in sequence either before or near the start of Lent is probably on balance the most appropriate place. But one must not overlook 6 August, provided it is backed up by the rich language of spiritual ascent and exposure to the 'uncreated light' that is such a hallmark of the Orthodox tradition, at once so different from the less ambitious tendency in the West to see the Transfiguration as a 'special experience' on a spiritual pilgrimage. This may well correspond to different views on how the narrative – and even the icon – is to be interpreted. Is it a matter of straight exposition, like that of John Chrysostom, Grundtvig, or Mark Frank? Or is it more allegorical, taking us into a far more complex world, as with Origen (c. 185–c. 245) and Gregory Palamas? Once again, history does not resolve any of these questions – nor should we expect it to do so. Yes, it's true that Byzantine icons grew out of the feast, but the ecumenical trade-route to the West now provides them with worlds for devotion and study that are different from their place of origin. And whether Transfiguration is seen as a narrative, a pivot on the way to Good Friday and Easter, or as a festival in August, it remains a crucial gateway to the central truths of our redemption.

Chapter 2

PROMISE

We shall make our way to Tabor, and see the tabernacles there which the Saviour shares, not as Peter wished, with Moses and Elijah, but with the Father and with the Spirit.

(Jerome, c. 345–420)[1]

'Truly I tell you, there are some standing here who will not taste death until they see that the Kingdom of God has come with power.'

(Mark 9:1)

'Truly I tell you, there are some standing here who will not taste death before they see the Son of Man coming in his Kingdom.'

(Matt. 16:28)

'But truly I tell you, there are some standing here who will not taste death before they see the Kingdom of God.'

(Luke 9:27)

A promise is a declaration made to another person about the future. Promises are given and received, but are often treated with suspicion. One of the main reasons for that suspicion is lack of trust. We often cynically talk of 'political promises', meaning things that we think we have to go through the motions of saying we will do, without really expecting to have to deliver anything to anyone else. And we can fall back on the old truth that we can predict everything except the future! Nonetheless, life as we know it needs collective disciplines for things to happen. A marriage survives times of tension because there is the will to keep going. A friendship persists because there is enough in common between two people for them to meet, even only occasionally after a gap of years, as if there had been no passage of time whatever. A public company can merge with another, because there is enough common purpose to work together, perhaps for the survival of the operation in the first place. But it can be otherwise: the marriage breaks down irretrievably; the friendship cannot survive the strain of too many misunderstandings; and the company-merger feels like a takeover, leaving behind a legacy of bitterness.

The icon by Theophanes holds together these separate worlds by the genius of the relationship between the upper world of Jesus and the lower world of the three disciples.[2] In one way, what is portrayed is the Transfiguration. But in another way, the entire painting chronicles each stage on the journey to the mountain-top and down again. By a subtle use of colours and distance, and the way the artist plays around with perspective, it is as if we can begin the whole drama with that strange promise that Jesus makes in front of the disciples, that *some* of them are in for something unusually special that is to do with the Kingdom of God. We shall discuss the subtle variants of the three narratives later, as well as Jerome's particular 'take' on the Transfiguration scene. But we can meanwhile ponder the tone of his words in a letter to a friend called Marcella written in 386 in which he tries to persuade her of the geographical beauty of the terrain, as well as the spiritual realities that Transfiguration means: not quite the tone of a travel brochure, but with a real sense of promise!

Theophanes and Jerome are on about the same thing: here is a God whom we can trust, because we can glimpse at his glory, a glory that is no optional extra, but impinges on the supposed 'real world', which may be a bit more brown than gold, but where the gold that is the background to Jesus' ministry lingers on, indelibly, in the ordinary living of discipleship.

So much for the promise of a by no means obvious outcome. What of those to whom the promise has been specifically given? Jesus is unambiguously clear: *some*, which means not others. Lying in a hospital bed having been suddenly diagnosed with acute leukaemia, all I could do was to trust in the promises of God, and rely on others to pray me through the biggest challenge of my life. I suppose my wrestling with those promises came down to trying to square the almost impossible circle of genetics – and providence. Why was it I who was struck down with the illness? And then, more pertinently, why was it I who had the genes to push me on my way towards remission, when someone in a neighbouring room, exactly the same age as me, did not survive? The 'some' of Jesus' promise took on a new meaning, and it is a meaning that mixed strangely with the modern, secular view that everyone is equal, with equal rights, which – therefore – ought to lead, somehow, to us all being treated the same. Our understanding of the strange ways of life and, if we believe, of the strange ways of God, make squaring that circle even more difficult. But one firm conviction emerged early on in my illness, which is that the world of righteous autonomy could give me no lasting answers whatever.

Be that as it may, scholars do differ on how restrictive that 'some' is. Christopher Evans interprets it to mean a large group,[3] whereas many years ago H. B. Swete accepted the fact that a strand of interpretation down the ages is not only restrictive, but means the three disciples taken by Jesus up the mountain.[4] The answer to that question lies in whether this verse, which appears in all three narratives, 'belongs' here or not. Either answer is possible. We can understand it to sum up teaching given by Jesus to the disciples about the cost of following him (Mark 8:27—9:1; Matt. 16:24–28; Luke 9:18–27), or else link this teaching closely with the Transfiguration, which is how Anastasius I Patriarch of Antioch (d. 598) treats the matter in an eloquent sermon on discipleship and the promise of redemption.[5] There does not seem to be a definitive answer: it depends on how the passage is 'read'. In the three gospel narratives, there is an 'inner cabinet' of Peter, James and John who keep recurring; and it is interesting to note the balance achieved. Matthew has them at the Transfiguration (Matt. 17:1) and also in Gethsemane (Matt. 26:37). Luke has them at the Transfiguration (Luke 9:28) and also both at the raising of Jairus's daughter (Luke 6:51) and to help prepare for the Passover (Luke 22:8). Mark uses them even more: at the Transfiguration (Mark 9:2), when Jairus's daughter is raised (Mark 5:37), in Gethsemane (Mark 14:23), but also at the top of the Mount of Olives when Jesus is about to enter Jerusalem (Mark 13:3). The inference is simple: this is a trusted group, from among the first called of the disciples.

Principles of selection are not always easy, and they continue to be part of public discussion at just about every level. The modern secular model is not always helpful, because it can be predicated on the false notion of 'fairness': everybody must be the same. But we aren't. Each of us has different gifts. As we shall see much later on (Chapter 9), it is something of a surprise to see just how Peter, James and John responded to being part of the Transfiguration: we might almost conclude from their behaviour that it doesn't seem to have done them much good! And yet Jesus chose them, hot-headed Peter, formerly called Simon, and the 'Sons of thunder' as he called James and John (Luke 5:10). From this it can be seen that they were the only disciples renamed, nicknamed, by Jesus. He could not take all twelve up the mountain, as that would have included Judas Iscariot. This point was made as long ago as the fourth century by Ephrem (c. 306–73), who wrote a commentary on an important second-century harmony of the four gospels by Tatian (*c.* 160) (called 'Tatian's *Diatessaron'*), which, significantly, regards this verse of promise as an integral part of the Transfiguration story.[6] Partly thanks to a lectionary that exposes us to all gospel-writers to an extent virtually unknown before, we tend to forget how the gospels were harmonised in the early centuries, either by such devices as the *Diatessaron*, or by preachers who went in for harmonising in their sermons.

The curious 'verse of promise' may well have its origin in a prediction by Jesus of the coming of the Kingdom. But placed here, it can just as easily refer to the Transfiguration scene, forming a bridge between his teaching about discipleship, and his deliberately selecting three already trusted companions to share with him in the mountain trek that was to lead to something extraordinary for all of them. It is interesting to observe a tendency to include this verse of promise in preaching-texts from the earliest times: John Chrysostom in Antioch in the 390s, as well as Cyril of Alexandria in the mid fifth century, although it is more prevalent in the West, starting with Hilary of Poitiers (*c.* 315–367/8) in the mid fourth century, Augustine of Hippo (354–430) in early fifth-century North Africa, as well as Jerome, as we shall see presently.[7] But it rarely appears later on, when the feast of Transfiguration on 6 August is established.[8] All these were influential figures, not regarded as eccentric or unusual. The Christ-figure of the icon beckons the chosen three, just as Jerome invites Paula, Eustochium and Marcella from his base in Bethlehem to come and join him near the sites and locations where Jesus lived and taught, in order to move beyond the physical places, and to become – in every sense – the 'audience' that participates in the gospels.

It will be clear by now that to the question, 'where does this verse belong?' there is no obvious answer. The drift of modern biblical scholarship detaches it from the Transfiguration narrative, and regards it as the conclusion of Jesus' teaching about the cost of discipleship and the coming of the Kingdom, in all three gospels. Nevertheless, that is not how it has been 'read' down the ages. So embedded is this prelude-verse in the memory of the Transfiguration scene that there are even examples of the verse being cited by preachers when it has not even been read. For our purposes, we have to take this persistent tradition seriously, without for one moment accepting the view that, whatever the precise origins of the verse, it blends well with both contexts: as the summation of Jesus' teaching, and as a lead-in to the Transfiguration. Scripture should not be treated in a wooden, unimaginative fashion, as if everything can only have one meaning, for fear that, if there might be some rich ambiguity, that would be in some sense a sell-out to pluralism and relativism.

So what of this verse of promise? As with the rest of the narrative, the variants are superficially minor, but in reality of some significance. Mark's version (Mark 9:1) reads in the original Greek as if it belongs with what follows rather than what precedes ('he also said'), whereas in Matthew and Luke, it is less clear.[9] All three use the expression 'taste death', which is not found in the Old Testament, but which perhaps comes across more graphically in English translation than in the original Greek, where it means 'die' (cf. John 8:52; Heb. 2:9). Nonetheless, the nuance is still there, as if a point were being made, over and above the act of dying. Attention is being deliberately drawn to the inevitable fact of death. Jesus is, perhaps, being depicted as rubbing this point home, an irony that the 'audience' of the gospel can only connect with his impending death.

This is a truth worth pausing for a moment to consider. The promise given is not meant to disguise the fact of death and dying. Even if its origins lie partly in a world that expected the imminent return of Jesus, the adjustment to its postponement, and the enduring, ongoing fact of Christian community in the ever-prolonged interim, meant that followers of Jesus had to get used to history as an unusual challenge. No longer could they expect Jesus to come again soon, but nor could they 'settle down' to the world as it is, with all its compromises and collusions. Those verses from Paul about being 'transfigured' into the image of Christ (2 Cor. 3:18), a process which begins by *not* being conformed to this world (Rom. 12:2), along with other similar passages show us that already the early Christians realised that the life of faith is about how we live now, where it is impossible to 'settle down' into history.

There is a cost to discipleship, and for some this means paying the biggest price of all, to give one's life in the process. To describe dying as 'tasting death' must, even in the background, have a sense that it must not be banished to the theoretical. When I was told about my illness, dying stopped being something that other people did, which would happen to me at some point when I was very old. It became a real possibility that stared me in the face. What I feared about dying was not the act itself, as I had been with people at that sacred moment often enough in the past. It was the prospect of leaving behind loved ones, who would have to do all sorts of practical things like get rid of all my books, to say nothing of the appalling pain of missing me once I'd gone. No wonder that night Sarah and I spoke together on the phone and agreed to help each other as we climbed this particular mountain, wherever it was going to lead.

'Some' will not 'taste death'. These might be anyone. In terms of the ensuing narrative, they are Peter, James and John, that inner cabinet of trusted intimates Jesus takes with him on the more special, delicate missions. But for the 'audience', for the friends of Jerome reading his letter of invitation, for the disciple gazing at the icon, they are anyone. It is not the specific task of the disciple to identify him- or herself with Peter, James and John, but rather with the whole drama, as if it were unfolding before us as we read it now. And each year, it may well be that the narrative is a slightly different one. So what do we make of it?

Mark's narrative we take first, and deliberately so, because it was in all probability the one which was written first. That goes against the grain of the three-year Lectionary, where Matthew is read in 'Year A'. But for our purposes, some critical attention to origins is important, particularly as Mark's is the shortest. So where Matthew has 'the Son of Man coming in his Kingdom', and Luke reads 'the Kingdom of God', Mark has the more explicit 'that the Kingdom of God has come with power'. Why these differences? When Mark is longer than the other two gospel-writers, we need to be ready to dig deeper. Mark, whose parables and healings are about the Kingdom of God, seems to want to portray Jesus here – yet again – as an enigma. Whereas Luke bluntly, and perhaps not a little ambiguously, describes the event simply as 'the Kingdom of God', and whereas Matthew describes it as process ('coming'), with Mark it is an event, complete, final, full. And yet with Mark there is always a sense that whatever happens will not be fully understood, and that the disciples will get the wrong end of the stick, and may even be scratching their heads as they try to make sense of something that has already happened, as if it has passed them by.

If we 'read' this verse of promise in the context of the Transfiguration, we are left with three somewhat different 'registers', three slightly different colorations to the icon as a narrative. Mark gives us a firm, established event that we are going to end up not fully understanding, long after it is over. Matthew points us to the future, to a process that will never end. And Luke makes us pause briefly on the way to the next stage in his carefully wrought, historical chronicle of the events of salvation. Of course, all three are predictions about the future, and, on their own, or seen in connection with their preceding verses, it is easy to see why they have been interpreted to refer to the Resurrection, the Second Coming, and even to the destruction of the temple in Jerusalem. But if we 'read' them as preludes to three different narratives of the Transfiguration, they speak of choice, of the reality of death, and of some kind of special event that will show something about the meaning and reality of Jesus of Nazareth that will be of enduring significance. Mark, usually the shortest of all, uses that word 'power' which in the New Testament means anything but the kind of assertive, forceful energy that we usually experience – and use – in this life. Matthew, the teacher's gospel, wants to claim the Jewish heritage, in this case, the coming 'Son of Man', for the new community. And Luke, often the idiosyncratic editor of the other two writers, unusually is the briefest of all three: 'the Kingdom of God' for Luke is to be part of the Christian story in a Gentile world.

Of all the writers in antiquity who have written on the Transfiguration, perhaps one of the most influential was Jerome (*c*. 345–420).[10] It is to him that we owe the determined project of producing an accurate Latin translation of the Bible, based on the best available Greek and Hebrew manuscripts, a 'popular' version subsequently completed after his death and nicknamed the 'Vulgate', on which all subsequent Latin versions in the Catholic Church have been based. Until 384 Jerome served as secretary to Pope Damasus (*c*. 304–84), who saw the need for such a translation, because of the many different Latin versions of varying quality that were in circulation. Jerome then returned to the East (he had received his ordination as a presbyter in Antioch) and eventually, in 386, settled in Bethlehem where he based all his subsequent work, as a preacher, scholar, and as a (sometimes sharp) correspondent.

Jerome's homilies were delivered in a conversational style. His homily on the Transfiguration uniquely is on the Marcan narrative, and he includes this verse of promise as the start.[11] From the very beginning, he strikes the note of judgement. 'There are many kinds of death: some taste death; others see death; still others eat it; some are glutted with it; others again are renewed by it. The apostles, on the contrary, because they were standing and were apostles, for that very reason did not

25

even taste death.' And he goes on to distinguish between tasting and seeing, in order to bring home the reality of dying, before turning back to the apostles: 'what He is actually saying is that they shall not die before they have seen Him ruling as King . . . When they saw Him transfigured upon the mountain, they saw Him in the glory that would be His.'

But already, he insinuates into his preaching a distinction between history and what he calls 'a spiritual explanation', by which he means an allegorical interpretation, following Origen (Chapter 9), by whom he was strongly influenced. That prepares him for the reason he gives for the choice of Peter, James and John as the three to whom this verse of promise is taken to refer: Peter is the Rock, on whom the Church is built (Matt. 16:18), James is the 'supplanter' (alluding to Jacob taking Esau's place, Gen. 27), and John because, according to Jerome, this means 'favour of the Lord'.[12] Jerome immediately turns to the spiritual reality of the Transfiguration, which is about ascent and transformation. But 'to this very day, Jesus is down below for some and up above for others. They who are below, the crowd who cannot climb the mountain, have Jesus down below – only the disciples climb the mountain, the crowd remains below – if anyone, I say, is one of the crowd, he cannot see Jesus in shining garments, only in soiled.'

Already we see Jerome sticking rigidly to Mark's narrative, referring to the Kingdom of God coming, and the garments shining, and no mention of Jesus' face (Mark 9:1, 3). There is no harmonisation of texts here, a trait of preaching we shall encounter in other figures. Jerome's spiritual (i.e., allegorical) treatment of the narrative identifies the shining garments with Holy Scripture – hence the importance of Jesus as the enlivening force for using the Bible. 'The earthly man cannot whiten his garments; but he who abandons the world and ascends the mountain with Jesus, and meditating mounts to heavenly contemplations, that man is able to make his garments white as no fuller on earth can do.'

This provides Jerome with an opportunity to draw attention

to the importance of some of his favourite themes: the letter kills, but the Spirit gives life, and if we have the Spirit, then we can 'penetrate Sacred Scripture'. That means reading the Old Testament (hence the presence of Moses and Elijah) in a way that is not carnal, 'down below, but if I grasp their spiritual significance, I am climbing to the top of the mountain'. When he comes to the three tents Peter is so keen to build (Mark 9:5), Jerome sees the Trinity encapsulated in them: 'unless I understand in the Trinity that will save me, no understanding can be sweet to me.' And almost inevitably, the voice (Mark 9:7) is interpreted christologically: 'this is my Son, of my nature, of my substance, abiding in me, and He is all that I am.'

A similar coverage is to be found in his *Commentary on St Matthew*, which he finished before Easter in 398.[13] Written in something of a hurry, there are signs here and there of impatience. For example, discussing the choice of the three disciples, he simply says that he's dealt with this often enough elsewhere. A treasure-trail leads back to another of his Homilies on Mark's gospel, where the 'inner cabinet' is mentioned for the first time (Mark 4:30–43, the raising of Jairus's daughter).[14] Here, Jerome goes to town on the matter. The three represent the Trinity; they correspond to the three peeled branches Jacob set in the watering-troughs (Gen. 30:38, in order to stimulate his flocks' reproductive activities, no less!); finally, and perhaps more specifically, Peter is chosen because the Church would be built on him, James is the first of the apostles to be martyred (cf. Acts 12:2), and John is the beloved disciple who prefigures the state of virginity. Of these last three, the reason for the choice of Peter is identical to what we read in his homily on the Transfiguration narrative, John's is a variant, whereas James's is new. In this, with or without Jacob as 'supplanter', Jerome is followed by a whole series of writers and preachers in the later West. This was given a boost with Bede (*c.* 673–735), another figure who mattered to scholars and preachers in the Middle Ages. He wrote a

sermon on the Matthew narrative, and (much more unusually) wrote commentaries on all the gospels.[15] As to
schemes for explaining the choice of the three disciples, we
shall see some other interpretations in the next chapter.

Jerome never loses a focus on the Transfiguration that
stresses its eschatological implications. His homily begins and
ends on the note of the Kingdom that is to come. Similarly, the
Commentary on St Matthew stresses that it is perceived by the
human senses, and is not something far away in the world of
dreams. Jesus does not lose his human form in the process, a
truth Jerome hammers out more graphically in his *Letter to
Pammachius* against John of Jerusalem, written around the
same time as the Matthew *Commentary* (398–99): 'Our Lord
was not so transfigured on the mountain that He lost his
hands and feet and other members, and suddenly began to
roll along in a round shape like that of a sun or a ball; but the
same member glowed with the brightness of the sun and
blinded the eyes of the apostles.'[16] And in the *Commentary*,
Jerome – ever one to try to get inside the human condition –
suggests three reasons for the apostles' fear: recognition of the
error in suggesting building three tents; the brightness of the
cloud (cf. 'blinded the eyes of the apostles' in the Letter just
quoted); and the fact that the divine Voice had spoken.

For Jerome, therefore, the Transfiguration is about Jesus
being revealed for what he is, and about discipleship being
illuminated for what it might lead to. At every stage, he has
an eye both for what Jesus is experiencing in terms of his
identity and mission, and what this must say about our
understanding of that for our stumbling following of him.
Transfiguration is about the Kingdom, at the end of time, but
it is about that Kingdom breaking in now. It is about spiritual
ascent, above the mundane world we know all too well. It is
about another ascent, from the familiar 'reading' of sacred
texts to a Christ-centred interpretation, where he is more than
a teacher, but *is* the message as well as the interpretation,
whether we are looking at the Old or the New Testaments.

Both belong in him. And if we are tempted, as Christians were in Jerome's day as much as today, to dismiss the Old Testament as somehow 'irrelevant' (to use a tired and well-tried put-down), then the answer comes back that there are hidden treasures to explore, as long as they are seen in the light of Christ himself. Moreover, Jerome, profound and learned biblical scholar that he was (he learnt Hebrew from a rabbi, a unique achievement for his time and culture), still communicates a sense that these explorations are not academic achievements for graduation, but far more mysterious avenues that it will take a lifetime to fathom – if then.

Even though we are in Bethlehem, so near to the sacred places which during Jerome's lifetime had become centres of pilgrimage, there is still no hint of a feast of Transfiguration. That is yet to come. But Jerome is among the first to identify Mount Tabor, a hill of a mere 1,843 feet not far from Nazareth as the location for this event, as his *Letter to Marcella* quoted earlier makes clear. The fourth century was a time for settling these matters. The historian Eusebius (*c.* 260–*c.* 340), commenting on the mention of Tabor and Hermon (Ps. 88:13), vaguely suggests that these were the places where the Transfiguration happened, whereas Cyril of Jerusalem (*c.* 315–87) regards the matter as settled. Towards the end of the sixth century, the Piacenza Pilgrim notes that there are three basilicas on Tabor, which is corroborated by Adamnán (*c.* 624–704), Abbot of Iona at the end of the following century. And Bede himself (though he never travelled there) writes that there was also a monastery.[17] All this suggests an understandable desire to locate the Transfiguration in a particular place, with the added advantage of combating any tendency to regard it as no more than a nice idea or an inward experience.

Each of the episodes in the Transfiguration narrative poses a question, and the question posed by this prelude verse of promise is 'when?' 'When will it all happen?' And the answer is always given by the reality of the event itself – which invariably leads on to something else, whether it is the next episode on the trek up the mountain or what we do with ourselves when we've returned. 'When' is the question of impatience, as it demands precision, as if the Kingdom of God – whether it is Mark's Kingdom, come in power, Matthew's Son of Man on the way, or Luke's bald statement of seeing it as it is – were tucked away in the appendix of a personal organiser. Once more, the contemporary, secular approach is less than adequate.

This prelude verse of promise can only set the scene for what follows. It can also be perceived in that icon, where the three are to be caught up in the extraordinary events at the top of the mountain. It is not for nothing that icon-painters, Theophanes the Greek included, show the three at the foot of the mountain, as if they have still the climb to undergo – as if the distance between them and Jesus is still considerable. The icon, therefore, does not depict a world already reconciled, as if everything were put right, and there are no problems. Rather the icon lives with the tensions of an unreconciled world – where the verse of promise still beckons and challenges. In the thirteenth century, Mechtild of Magdeburg (c. 1207–82), one of the foremost women writers of her time, speaks of the distance between ourselves and God, and how God is determined to bridge it himself, in a way that combines the images of the mountain, the cornfield and the bride. It is that distance, and the mercy that reaches towards us, which lies at the heart of this verse of promise.

> Lord, my sin because of which I have lost you
> Stands before my eyes like a huge mountain,
> Creating between us
> Darkness and distance.
> O Love, above all love,
> Draw me to yourself again.
>
> But Lord, the prospect of future falls
> Plagues my mind:

They beckon to me like the mouth of a fiery dragon
Eager to swallow me whole.
O my only Good, help me now
That I may flow sinless towards you.

Lord, my earthly being lies before me
As an acre of dust
On which little good has grown.
O sweet Jesus Christ,
Send me now the fruitful rain of your humanity,
And the gentle dew of the Holy Spirit
That I may plead my heart's sorrow.

Your everlasting kingdom
Lies open before my eyes
Like a wedding feast,
Inviting me to your everlasting banquet.
O true lover
Never cease to draw to your side this lovesick bride.
All the gifts I have ever received from you
Stand before me as a heavy reproach
For this your highest gift humbles me to the dust.

Then God who gives us everything answered thus:
'Your mountain of darkness shall be melted away by my
    love,
Your enemies shall win no victory over you,
Your acre has been scorched by the rays of the hot sun
Yet its fruit has not been destroyed.
In my kingdom you will live as a new bride,
There I will greet you with the kiss of love
And all my Godhead shall sweep through your soul;
My three-fold being shall play ceaselessly
In your two-fold heart.
What place then has mourning?
If you were to pray for a thousand years
I would never give you cause
For a single sigh.'[18]

31

Chapter 3

ASCENT

In all supernatural works we rather draw back than help on.
(John Hacket, 1590–1670)[1]

Six days later, Jesus took with him Peter and James and John, and led them up a high mountain apart, by themselves.
(Mark 9:2)

Six days later, Jesus took with him Peter and James and his brother John and led them up a high mountain, by themselves.
(Matt. 17:1)

Now about eight days after these sayings, Jesus took with him Peter and John and James, and went up on the mountain to pray.
(Luke 9:28)

Traprain Law is a hill about nine hundred feet high, which dominates the skyline of the coastal part of East Lothian, south of the main road between Haddington and Dunbar. A geological accident, it is nowadays a place for country walks and sheep. From the summit on a fine day one can get a fair sight northwards across the Firth of Forth to Fife, southwards to the Lammermuir Hills, eastwards out to the North Sea, and westwards to Edinburgh. Not being the world's greatest mountaineer, I only once climbed Traprain as a boy, in company with a couple of friends. At first, we walked closely together, talking about the climb ahead. But gradually, it became steeper. So we began to stick to the sheep-tracks that seemed to have been there from time immemorial. On we went in single file, and the steeper the climb became, the more zigzag-like became the walk. Because we were young and inexperienced, every time we reached the summit of part of the hill, we thought we'd got to the top, and every time disappointment took over in the face of such apparent deceit. At long last, we reached the top, and the sense of achievement was palpable, as the picnic was opened, and we scoured the horizon for all the sights that were so familiar, albeit from more normal ground level.

It's not surprising that mountains have figured so prominently in people's experiences across the centuries. People have been enchanted by them, either as challenges to climb, particularly, as with Tenzing and Hillary on Mount Everest in 1953, if they have summits known never to have been reached before. Mountains and hills provide opportunities for detachment from the familiar world. The trek together of a group has the habit of binding them together, even – perhaps especially – in the silence of a single-file walk. It is perhaps a bit of a surprise that in a talkative age like ours people can get to know each other just as easily through silence as through a conversation. Moreover, mountains and hills have their own climates. Clouds can suddenly descend, and change those perspectives quite quickly, so that distances that were a few moments ago clear and familiar become skewed and the echoes produced by different voices that were once familiar and predictable quickly develop less familiar and less predictable resonances, because the mist is so heavy. All one can do is go on to the end. You don't have to be religious to like mountain-tops, but some religious people appreciate some-times being up there, away from it all.

For the first 'audiences' of the gospels, that mountain-trek up to the Transfiguration could not fail to evoke memories from Israel's past, which was full of mountains. There is Mount Sinai, also known as Mount Horeb, where the People of Israel encamped for a whole year (Exod. 19:1, 18; Deut. 4:10). Tradition identifies it as Jebel Musa in southern Sinai, quite a climb at 7,363 feet. At its feet lies the monastery of St Catherine, founded by the Emperor Justinian *c.* AD 527, sup-posedly on the site of a church built by the Emperor Con-stantine's mother, Helena, two centuries earlier, during the time when the holy places were being identified and given churches to commemorate the special events associated with them. It is here that Moses is supposed to have ascended, with the seventy elders, and with three trusted companions, Aaron, Nadab and Abihu, in order to confirm the covenant (Exod. 24:1). It is here that Moses ascended in order to speak with God, but not to see him (Exod. 24:12–18); God's glory covered the mountain in a cloud for six days, and Moses was given the substance of the covenant between God and the People of Israel (Exod. 25—31). As Davies and Dale Allison remark, 'one strongly suspects that the informed reader is to recall this Old Testament text.'[2]

But it is one thing to see significant parallels in the Old Testament, and the collective memory of the People of Israel. It is another to see the distinctiveness of the Transfiguration, as an event in its own right. The truth of its Old Testament setting may lie in the linking of Moses and Elijah,[3] not just when one recalls that it is both of them who appear on the mountain. On the way down, the disciples ask Jesus about the coming of Elijah (Mark 9:11–13; Matt. 17:10–13; not in Luke – see Chapter 9), whom they had just apparently seen on the mountain-top speaking with Jesus. But it is not just Moses who is associated with Mount Sinai. Elijah fled here in order to escape persecution (1 Kings 19:4–18), and it was here that he saw God not in the wind, nor the earthquake, nor the fire, but in a 'sound of sheer silence' (1 Kings 19:12; cf. RSV 'still small voice'), an experience that leads Elijah from total dejection to the anointing of Hazael and Jehu as kings of Syria and Israel, and of Elisha as his successor (1 Kings 19:15–18).

Sinai in the cold, dry south provides one important point of context, associated with such formative figures as Moses and Elijah. But the hills and mountains surrounding the Sea of Galilee are more immediate, in particular those abutting the fertile valley of Jezreel. First there is Mount Tabor, compared with Sinai a mere stripling at 1,843 feet, a cone-shaped hill about five miles west of Nazareth; because of its size, and proximity to the traditional place of Jesus' upbringing, it is not surprising that it was a winner in finding a location for the Transfiguration. (Just over twice the height of Traprain Law, but still no more than an afternoon's climb!) It is mentioned in Old Testament prophecy (Jer. 46:18; Hos. 5:1), as well as in psalmody, along with Mount Hermon (Ps. 88:12). Deborah and Barak came down upon the Canaanites and defeated them (Judg. 4—5). Mount Moreh (1,815 feet), five miles to the south of Tabor, was the campsite of the Midianites when attacked by Gideon (Judg. 7:1), and not far is Nain, where Jesus raised from the dead the widow's son (Luke 7:11–17). Not far away, to the south-west, is the Mount Carmel range (the central part reaches 1,790 feet). It was here that Elijah and the prophets of Baal had their public confrontation over the production of rain (1 Kings 18), which led to Jezebel's re-taliation against Elijah, and Elijah's flight southwards to Mount Sinai (1 Kings 19), referred to earlier.

We can probably dismiss Tabor as the location of the Transfiguration, and go for one of the spurs of Mount Her-mon, which at 9,230 feet was a good six-hour climb.[4] The fact of the matter is that none of the evangelists seems interested in identifying the mountain, and it wasn't until the fourth century when 'holy geography' came into vogue that Tabor emerged as the winner. But even if we live with that early identification, there is still that bank of special associations of hills and mountains in the Old Testament. First and foremost must come Sinai, a special place for both Moses and Elijah. Then there are the mountains and hills of Jezreel, including Tabor, which must have had their own local charm for at least some of the first Christians, especially those who, from the fourth century onwards, used Luke's gospel in developing the liturgical year and calendar.[5] And finally, Mount Carmel, site of Elijah's final and most public confrontation with his clerical rivals, the prophets of Baal, provides a dimension of real conflict, which cannot be overlooked, given Jesus' recent predictions about suffering and death, and the cost of following him (Mark 8:31–38; Matt. 16:21–26; Luke 9:21–26).

Something of this jumble of mountains and hills is conveyed eloquently by Theophanes the Greek in the Transfiguration icon. Indeed, as Andreopoulos has shown, there does not seem to be much of a desire in the Byzantine iconographic tradition to paint a single, identifiable mountain.[6] For him, as with some other late medieval artists, the actual mountain climb is portrayed in the small vignette on the left-hand side, between Elijah and Peter, who are above and below, respectively. The four figures are depicted in single file, with Jesus looking slightly backwards at his three companions, his halo underlining his identity. There is a strong sense of purposeful, if slightly fatigued *movement* in that little scene, as if drawing attention, in all its smallness, to the essential part of the whole narrative which it is portraying – getting together to the top. We as the 'audience' of the narrative are drawn to its fullest implications.

When it comes to the three narratives, the variants are once again significant. All three are at one that Jesus took the three up a mountain, but the differences are principally that whereas Mark and Matthew record that this took place after six days, Luke has 'now about eight days after these sayings'. As Heil maintains, all three are agreed that there is a relationship between the Transfiguration and the teaching about discipleship and the coming suffering and death of Jesus, but there is also the sense of a break. 'What is about to happen occurs nearly a week later, indicating the initiation of a new and separate event.'[7] Indications of time are not common in the gospels, so we are left to conclude that it is given here in order to point up the significance of what is to follow. Commentators from the earliest times, too, have done their best to harmonise the Mark/Matthew 'six' with the Lucan 'about eight'. On the one hand, it would be easy to say that they mean roughly the same thing. Such a functional, surface interpretation has much to commend it. Because of the centrality given to Matthew's account, early writers tended to draw attention to Luke's 'eight' in passing, and suggest that 'after six' means some kind of symbolic Sabbath, whereas the 'eight' expresses completion, pointing to the resurrection, a new age altogether. This is the line taken by Ambrose of Milan (c. 339–97), in one of the few commentaries on Luke's gospel in antiquity, which was read by Bede, as well as Carolingian writers such as Druthmar (d. c. 880), Rabanus Maurus (c. 780–856) and Paschasius Radbertus (c. 790–c. 860). Ambrose subtly weaves in the resurrection not only in terms of Jesus' own rising from the dead, but as an 'eternal fruit' that we ourselves await. He thus lifts the Transfiguration way above the level of the mundane. He also provides three explanations for the choice of the three disciples: Shem, Ham and Japheth, the sons of Noah (Gen. 5:32), thus embracing the entire human race, all believers, and the Trinity.[8]

The other main variant, picked up by many preachers (and commentators) is Luke's focus on *prayer* as the purpose of the expedition (Luke 9:28). (Luke's preference for placing John before James – already at 8:51 as well – probably results from John's closeness to Peter [cf. Acts 3:1; 8:14], which need not detain us.) We have already drawn attention to the importance of Jesus praying at important stages in Luke's gospel narrative: at his baptism (Luke 3:21), before calling the disciples (Luke 6:12), before asking them about his identity (Luke 9:18), in Gethsemane (Luke 22:40f: paralleled in Matt. 26:36; Mark 14:32), and when he prays for forgiveness of those who are responsible for his crucifixion while it is being carried out (Luke 23:34). But, as Evans points out, in relation to the following verse, 'while he was praying' (Luke 9:29), there is no assumption in Luke that Transfiguration was the purpose of the mountain trek: rather, it is imposed on Jesus as he prays.[9] And Lee even uses the motif of Jesus at prayer as a way of underscoring his solitude, and the silence of the disciples at the end in contrast to the great experience that has just taken place.[10] There can be little doubt that the repeated references to Jesus praying are intended to heighten his relationship with the Father, and the Transfiguration is certainly a manifestation of precisely that relationship.

None of the gospel-writers, as we have said, identifies the mountain. Luke locates the narrative at the end of the Galilee ministry (Luke 4:14—9:50) and as a prelude to the arduous journey to Jerusalem (Luke 9:51—19:28), but even that gives no clue as to its whereabouts. Of all the three gospel-writers, it is Matthew who uses the mountain theme most: the devil took Jesus to 'a very high mountain' to tempt him (Matt. 4:8); Jesus preached from 'the mountain' (Matt. 5:1), and came down from it at the end (Matt. 8:1); he dismisses the crowds and goes up 'the mountain' to pray by himself (Matt. 14:23); he goes up 'the mountain' and sits down in order to heal the sick (Matt. 15:29); after the Transfiguration, in his teaching about faith, Jesus refers to the possibility of moving 'this mountain' (Matt. 17:20); and at the end, the disciples go to Galilee, to 'the mountain' to which Jesus directed them (Matt. 28:6) for Jesus' parting words. Some of these instances appear in Mark and Luke, but not to anything like this extent.

But there is nothing like the obvious parallels between Jesus and Moses that we find in Matthew in terms of his teaching, not just the Sermon on the Mount (Matt. 5—7), but what is sometimes called the Missionary Discourse (Matt. 10), the parables (Matt. 13), the Community Rules (Matt. 18), and the Discourse about the End (Matt. 24—25). All this surrounds the Transfiguration, and turns into a kind of new Mount Sinai in a way that is not nearly so much the case with Mark and Luke. Moreover, the 'after six days' is another Sinai touch, for Moses ascended Sinai, and the cloud descends on him for six days, and the Lord speaks to him, and only on the seventh does he enter the cloud, and climb to the summit, where he stays forty days (Exod. 24). We are left to the conclusion that there is in Matthew a deliberate emphasis on and sequence of moun- tains, both for good things (Jesus teaching and healing) as well as bad (Jesus being tempted), that Jesus is the new Lawgiver, who supersedes Moses, not only in what he teaches, but in how he experiences the Father directly on that mountain-top – whose identity, unlike Sinai, is of no apparent consequence. For Luke, mountains are not important at all, and all the more so because Jesus' main block of teaching takes place on level ground, on the plain (Luke 6:20–end). Although, as we have pointed out already, ancient tradition associates the mount of Transfiguration with Tabor, a likely, local Galilean candidate, that does not prevent Sinai recurring as a motif in the sermon by Anastasius, Abbot of Sinai (d. *c.* 700) (not to be confused with Anastasius, Patriarch of Antioch, d. 598), who preached one of the first sermons known to have been delivered on the Feast of the Transfiguration to his monastic community, right under the magnificent mosaic depicting the scene, towards the end of the sixth century.[11]

All three narratives use the same word for 'take' (really meaning 'take along'). This is the same word used of the devil 'taking' Jesus up the very high mountain in order to tempt him (Matt. 4:8). As Heil points out,[12] Jesus tells the devil to get behind him (Matt. 4:10); and when Peter 'took him aside' in order to question his prediction about suffering and death, Jesus rebukes him with similar words, 'get behind me' (Matt. 16:21–23). All this may suggest another pattern of 'getting behind' Jesus, namely of following him, in the immediately ensuing scene, of following him up the mountain. The Transfiguration narrative can thus be invested with more meaning still: 'took along with him' is decisive not only about the three, but about the trip itself. We are not talking about a chance country stroll. Jesus decided to go, and he decided very definitely who should come with him, chosen disciples who were there to follow behind him.

Then there is Mark's tiny assertive addition, 'apart'. That serves to emphasise his particular use of the 'inner cabinet', marginally more frequent in his gospel than in the other two. It also serves to underline that the trip is going to be a special one. In the language of participation, the 'audience' is prepared for something unusual that is to follow; to gaze at the icon means being drawn into an event of some significance. As Leo the Great (d. 461) puts it in his Lenten Sermon:

> For the unspeakable and unapproachable vision of the Godhead itself, which is reserved till eternal life for the pure in heart, they could in no wise look upon and see while still surrounded with mortal flesh. The Lord displays His glory, therefore, before chosen witnesses, and invests that bodily shape which He shared with others with such splendour, that His face was like the sun's brightness and His garments equalled the whiteness of snow.[13]

But there is a deeper, more penetrating theme which is taken up by two of the greatest preachers of antiquity, John Chrysostom (c. 347–407) and Augustine (c. 354–420). Referring to the disciples' fear immediately after the Transfiguration (Matt. 17:6), Chrysostom asks, rhetorically, 'how then did they fall down?' and he comes up with the reply, 'because there was solitude, and height, and great quietness'.[14] And Augustine in one sermon remarks, somewhat earthily, that Peter was finding the crowds a dreadful bore, and had discovered the solitude of the mountain; and in another sermon he explains Peter's desire to build three tents as a pretext for remaining up there: 'Peter was delighted with the solitude, he had grown tired of the turbulent, troublesome human race.'[15] For both Chrysostom and Augustine, the mountain is clearly a place of solitude, refuge, spiritual detachment and perspective; and Chrysostom's 'quietness' (*hēsuchia*) becomes in the Byzantine tradition an all-important spiritual quality in monasticism, which we shall come across with Gregory Palamas and the role of 'hesychasm' in relation to the Transfiguration (see Chapter 7). Returning to the question of the 'inner cabinet', it is interesting to note that whereas Augustine passes over it in silence, Chrysostom suggests that Peter was chosen because he loved Jesus the most, John because he was beloved by Jesus, and James because he was to be put to death (Acts 12:2).

Many are the writers and preachers who could have been chosen for special treatment at this stage of the narrative. Jerome is a well-known celebrity, John Hacket somewhat less so. He was born in 1592 and attended Westminster School at the same time as the future priest-poet George Herbert (1593–1633), while Lancelot Andrewes (1555–1626), one of the greatest preachers of the early Stuart era, was Dean of Westminster.[16] From there he went on to study at Trinity College, Cambridge, and was ordained in 1618. He served as Vicar of St Andrew's, Holborn, London, from 1624 until 1645. He retained his other cure at Cheam (in those days it was quite normal to have more than one parish, with assistant clergy to help). St Andrew's, Holborn was a significant place, and it would not do at that time for someone who in any way favoured Charles I to remain in such a post. At the Restoration of the monarchy in 1660, he was appointed a Canon Residentiary of St Paul's Cathedral, and in the following year, Bishop of Coventry and Lichfield, where he remained until his death in 1670 – and where his lasting legacy was a rebuilding of Lichfield Cathedral.

Five years later, in 1675, a collection of a hundred of his sermons was published. He liked giving extended courses of sermons, whether on the baptism of Christ or the temptations in the wilderness. Not quite halfway through come no fewer than seven on the Transfiguration.[17] This is the largest and most extensive preaching coverage of the Transfiguration that has come down to us: Gregory Palamas, enthusiast that he is for the festival, manages two, while Augustine produces three, the third of which is only a couple of paragraphs. More significantly, although Hacket refers to the other two gospel narratives in these sermons, he chooses the Lucan version as his base. He begins the first sermon by coming straight to the point: 'because St Luke doth more completely narrate all the circumstances of our Saviour's Transfiguration than the other Evangelists, therefore I have chosen to entreat out of his words that glorious miracle.'[18] This becomes something of an Anglican trait, as we shall discover with Mark Frank (Chapter 6), and finds its contemporary expression in that whereas modern Anglican revisions use all three versions in turn in the 'narrative' reading of Transfiguration before Lent (following the ecumenical adaptation of the three-year lectionary), they opt for Luke only for the 'festal' reading on 6 August.

But there is one more peculiarity to Hacket's treatment. He knows about the feast, and he also knows about the Lenten tradition as well. But he believes Transfiguration belongs to Eastertide, and should therefore be preached about during that season, thus giving it a Resurrection flavouring. The 6 August commemoration was abolished at the English Reformation and, except in the Calendar, did not reappear in the revision of the Prayer Book in 1662. All in all, these sermons could only have been preached by a vicar to his regular flock over a series of seven Sundays. On one occasion he mentions the dedication of the church in which he is preaching as St Andrew.[19]

Hacket's sermons are an astonishing find for the contemporary reader. They lack the concise style of Jerome or

Augustine, but they are deeply learned, with references both to ancient writers, like Origen and Chrysostom, medievals like Aquinas, as well as Reformation figures such as Luther and Calvin. Clearly influenced by Andrewes in the way he connects Christian truths together, the sermons come in a style that would have appealed to a congregation of London intelligentsia such as would have gathered from the legal and other professions in Holborn at that time. They have a directness and a clarity of structure, which means that the reader, the contemporary 'audience', knows where they are being led. In the first sermon (on Luke 9:28–29),[20] he connects the preceding verse of promise (Luke 9:27) with the three disciples (his patristic reading would have provided this). In a bluff, knock-down manner that comes across when he deals with other intricate points, he maintains that the 'six days' of Mark and Matthew mean exactly the same thing as Luke's 'eight days'. But his reasoning is not superficial: 'when outwardly there seems to be some disagreement between the text of one Evangelist and another, these difficulties do whet our industry to study the book of God: there must be knots and mysteries hard to be understood.'

When it comes to the identity of the mountain, he calls in Bernard of Clairvaux (1090–1153), who in one of his sermons on the Ascension exhorts the Christian to ascend not one but two mountains, the one where Jesus taught (Matt. 5—7) and the mountain of Transfiguration (Matt. 17:1–9).[21] Hacket is not overly interested in the Tabor tradition, which, though he accepts, he regards as a distraction, preferring a more direct interpretation that can reach people. 'A valley is as capable of God's glory as a mountain', but Jesus chose a 'high hill' for his prayer, as well as 'for the mystery of his transformation'. Then he explains himself: 'upon the higher ground there is the more free contemplation of heaven, the place to which we lift up our eyes and our hearts in prayer . . . Next our Saviour left a concourse of people beneath, and went to the mountain to pour out his devotions there in a solitary sequestration, where he should not be troubled.' We must start with 'the mountain of obedience' (the Sermon on the Mount) before we 'run on presumptuously upon the assurance of glorification' (the Transfiguration).

Next, Hacket deals with the choice of the three disciples. These sermons were probably preached some time in the 1630s in a capital city where the kind of Reformed Christianity which the nation was espousing was still under some debate. There was a genuine fear of Roman Catholicism in many quarters. It is therefore no surprise that Hacket should immediately dispel any notion that Peter had some kind of 'supremacy'. (Hacket jests about what Luther or Calvin might have said.) But Peter was not taken on his own: he went with two others. Why, then, this choice? Following patristic tradition, he cites the Trinity, both of the disciples ('Christ did not exceed that mystical number'), and of the Transfiguration itself ('Christ in visible splendour, the Father in the voice, the Holy Ghost in the bright cloud'), echoing a mannerism in Andrewes' preaching. And like Andrewes, Hacket sees the connection with Christ's baptism (Mark 1:9–11; Matt. 3:16–17; Luke 3:21–22).[22] But when it comes specifically to the three, Hacket produces his own variant of what we have seen already: 'Peter is more noted in the book of Acts than any of the Twelve for performing miracles: James was the first among the Twelve that suffered martyrdom; and John was the eagle that soared highest of them in his doctrine and divinity.' He leaves the question open as to 'their aptness', and goes on to suggest that, although there are no records in the gospels that Andrew minded not being included, even though he was the first to be called, and even brought Simon Peter to Jesus (John 1:40), we might have thought that he would have been in their number. But not all the twelve could have been included in any case, because that would have meant taking Judas Iscariot along, a point made particularly in the Eastern tradition, starting as early as Ephrem the Syrian (c. 306–73), and continued thereafter with Proclus of Constantinople

(d. 446), Anastasius of Antioch (d. 598), and John of Damascus (*c.* 655–*c.* 750), the source noted by Hacket.[23]

In the end, Hacket observes that the choice probably lay in their spiritual capacity, a view we have encountered already, and he links this with Luke's view that Jesus went up there in order to *pray*. That is why he remarks that 'in all supernatural works we rather draw back than help on.' For Hacket, expounding the Transfiguration to a congregation for whom it was not a familiar feast, it would have been tempting to treat it as a 'special experience', and no more. Instead, he keeps hold of the contemplative aspect of the Christian faith, seeing the summit of the mountain in terms of liturgical worship. Drawing a parallel with the Jewish Temple, he points to the central actions of the Church: 'instead of the Table of Shewbread we have the Communion of Christ's Body and Blood, the Table of the Lord. And instead of the altar of incense we have that which is much sweeter in God's nostrils, the incense of prayer.' And we are led on to what happened on the mountain-top, where he uses his own allegory about Christ's garments: they apply to *us*, as 'the robe of sanctity' (the baptismal robe), 'the robe of justification' ('it reacheth over all'), and 'the robe of glory' (eternal life).[24] Hacket's overall treatment is both rich and comprehensive, combining practical exposition with a strong sense of the history of interpretation – including an acceptance of the place of allegory.

There is one course of action which is very difficult to do on a mountain-trek of any kind, and that is turning back. No mountaineer likes giving up. And it is the same when embarking on any kind of journey. Lying in a hospital bed undergoing a course of chemotherapy is not dissimilar. There is a – theoretical – choice of giving up. There is also an increasing sense that the whole schedule of treatment has taken over one's life. And there is the added dimension of surrendering control altogether, and never quite knowing where the journey is going to lead, how grim and lonely some parts of it are going to be, and how it is going to end, as one is deprived of so much that is familiar, and surrenders to being in the hands of other people, whether they are nurses, doctors, God himself.

All key journeys of any significance 'take over', and become the presenting influence, the dominant force. And just as the question 'when?' is posed by the challenge of promise, so the question 'where?' is posed by the challenge of ascent. Where is Jesus taking us? It is another very secular quest, if – that is – it is to be answered in precise detail before embarking on the journey. When I agreed to be Bishop of Portsmouth in the summer of 1995, I had no idea where the journey would lead me, whatever it was – to two periods of sick leave in order to undergo treatment for leukaemia, during much of which time I felt utterly useless, or to dealing with some of the crises that are part of the job. Whatever mountain it was that Jesus 'took' his disciples up, the journey gathered its own momentum, regardless of what might or might not happen at the summit, simply because Jesus led the way. The journey can be of any kind, provided that it is about something important. The temptation for us is to undermine its importance, and keep it superficial, on the level of convenience-packed food, like the church meeting that wants to discuss the cost of flowers rather than what the reality of redemption might mean today. Hacket was right when he said that we 'draw back' rather than 'help on' when faced with the supernatural.

Portsmouth is not known for its mountain peaks, though there is a spectacular view across to the Isle of Wight from Portsdown Hill. It is a place, rather, that is dominated by the sea. In 1588, a time when religious and political forces took over international relations, when the Spanish Armada threatened England with invasion, because Spain was Roman Catholic and England was Protestant, and when Catholics were persecuting Protestants on Continental Europe with as much enthusiasm as Protestants were persecuting Catholics in England, Sir Francis Drake commended the task of defending his country through naval power to the mercy of God. The prayer that has been formed from his words has a far wider application, and could be used as easily by any Christian, regardless of their allegiance. The passage of time – like a mountain – can provide its own distance and perspective. There is an energy and determination of 'ascent' in the Francis Drake prayer:

> O Lord God, when thou givest to thy servants to endeavour any great matter, grant us also to know that it is not the beginning, but the continuing of the same, until it be thoroughly finished, which yieldeth the true glory; through him who for the finishing of thy work laid down his life for us, our Redeemer, Jesus Christ.[25]

Chapter 4

CHANGE

With a flashing wreath up on the summit
The Transfigured Jesus stood.
It warmed us right inside
To the deepest roots of our hearts.

(N. F. S. Grundtvig, 1783–1872)[1]

And he was transfigured before them, and his clothes became
dazzling white, such as no one on earth could bleach them.

(Mark 9:3)

And he was transfigured before them, and his face shone like the
sun, and his clothes became dazzling white.

(Matt. 17:2)

And while he was praying, the appearance of his face changed,
and his clothes became dazzling white.

(Luke 9:29)

Queen Elizabeth II has probably one of the best-known faces in the world. She also has had more than her fair share of portraits painted of her – a rough guess is two per year since her reign began over fifty years ago. In the run-up to her eightieth birthday celebrations in 2006, the famous Australian media personality Rolf Harris was commissioned to add to this list. There was much huffing and puffing in the artistic world, because Rolf was seen as a populariser and not really a full member of their club. He even had a television programme about the way the portrait emerged, complete with the subject's presence – and participation! The British Royals are notoriously tight-lipped about their portraits, but the Queen did manage to let slip that she thought the result made her look 'friendly'. Whatever the lasting assessment that time will make of the Harris painting, the programme probably brought home to people who watched it the sheer complexity and subtlety of what goes into a portrait. And it was made particularly clear at one point when the viewer saw the Queen sitting next to the emerging painting. On the left side was the 'real thing', and on the right was the beginnings of something different, with all the care that went into getting the right shade of green for the dress, and the right angles in the teeth to project a smile. The portrait produces a change in appearance, a 'trans-figuration'.

Often the two most significant aspects of a portrait are the face and the main clothing, as these are usually the most immediate keys to recognition. With the Rolf Harris painting, there was little need with such a well-known face, but the dress chosen (by him) was a key to the atmosphere of the personality he was trying to interpret. There was something of the nation's grandmother in the result, a quite proper interpretation. With other, more complex portraits, clothing and 'props' might be more important. This explains why, shortly after I was made a bishop, when someone approached me to paint my portrait, it was a good idea for me to be wearing something like the Anglican episcopal scarlet-and-white outfit, and a piece of good, clean family fun for me to have my grandfather's pulpit Bible beside me. Such 'props' don't tell the whole story, but they help to say something about the person concerned.

49

When it comes to deciding which is more important, clothing or face, face will always in the end win. Clothing may describe role, and the way the clothing is shown could even say something about how the subject 'wears' that role: not a few portraits betray signs of unease between the wearer and the role. But it's the face that says most – even if what is said is concealed. Like someone who keeps a daily diary but still manages to hide from any future reader (themselves?) what they are really thinking and feeling, a portrait can provide no more than a mask. Even with people who, for example, have very noticeable mannerisms or disabilities, the face is what 'says' most: eyes, mouth, teeth, hair (of lack of it), eyebrows, the angle of the head in relation to the neck (another potential giveaway for a person's sense of ease or unease). We never talk of recognising someone much by anything except their faces, because that is 'how they look'. Paintings, and portraits in particular, often engender a sense of real encounter with the onlooker. This is why, for example, George Steiner is so keen to help us see that art, along with music and poetry, can help us 'relate most directly to that in being which is not ours'.[2]

It may well be for these reasons that Eastern iconography spent much of the twentieth century developing an influence far outside the confines of Eastern Orthodoxy. Western Christians may not approach icons with quite the spiritual disciplines and theological interpretations which their Eastern sisters and brothers have learnt over the centuries. That may result in the occasional break in communication. The Eastern Christian would shrink from likening an icon to a portrait, because they would say that an icon is far, far more: it is a likeness, but it is more than that, not because of what it is in itself, but because it is supposed to lead us on to help us pray to God in the particular context of the figure or figures in the scene that has been painted. That is why there are conventions about where certain icons should be placed, as well as how they are painted. And that is why special icons are brought out on feast days for the faithful to come and venerate.

The same is true of the Transfiguration.[3] On 6 August, an icon of the *Metamorphōsis* will be placed in a prominent position. And it will, obviously, be 'recognised' by the scene which it portrays, principally the figure of Christ. Even though we do not know what Jesus really looked like (recent attempts to 'recreate' him are at some variance from the popular Turin Shroud likenesses of recent Western tradition), there are conventions that help the overall family of likenesses to cohere: 'that must be Jesus there'. But still it cannot be a portrait, because the purpose of Transfiguration icons is to portray Jesus in a particular context. It is the 'props' that give the story away, in this case a mountain, two figures on either side of him, and three below, and devices like a mandorla and rays of light to differentiate this particular scene in Jesus' life from others, like his baptism or resurrection, which it resembles, and to which it bears some relation.

Iconography needs these 'props', and rightly so. They help us to see why we are looking at this particular icon, whether it has been brought out for the August festival, or whether it is part of a series depicting the life of Christ on the iconostasis ('icon-stand') that marks out the place between the sanctuary and the rest of the church. But even though the face of Christ is in some sense 'unknown', his face remains of profound importance for the icon, for it brings home to the worshipper that he has a personal identity, however mysterious. As many a Transfiguration sermon is at pains to point out, the Christ of Transfiguration is at one and the same time the earthly man and the Son of God, the two natures of Christ coexisting, indivisible. Leo the Great refers to 'the changeless Godhead' in the Transfiguration.[4] It is another reason why Paul exhorts his hearers to preach Christ Jesus as Lord, 'for it is the God who said, "Let light shine out of darkness", who has shone in our hearts to give the light of the knowledge of the glory of Christ in the face of Jesus Christ' (2 Cor. 4:5–6).

But – and it is a big 'but' – we are still left with our own faces. I found myself living in a hospital room on and off for some time, the first stay (of just over four weeks) being the longest. During that time, I was cut off from a great deal that was familiar. The daily routine consisted of learning new faces, whether it was the regular round for blood-pressure, pulse, oxygen in the blood, and the temperature (when trying to throw off an infection, this was the most important of all). Lying in bed, it was always the *face* of the nurse or the doctor, or Sarah, or the family, or friends, that I looked at first. And I always found myself trying not to look at how my face registered with them, especially at the beginning. I tried not to try to interpret how ill I might have looked on that particular day, in case of disappointment. And then I began to realise that there might be a reason why the mirrors in those rooms were so small – to prevent me looking into them in order to see how I really looked. Chemotherapy has a way of 'transfiguring' one's face, not beyond recognition, but certainly beyond the boundaries of how I have looked before. My face mattered, whereas my clothing – pyjamas! – mattered little.

The kind of transfiguration I am really describing is not the professionally skilled distortions that might go into a portrait, like Winston Churchill looking pompous, or Charles I looking regal and majestic for the sake of effect, nor the deliberate over-exaggerations of a cartoon, like portrayals of the Prime Minister or the President of the Unites States of America, as these might appear in the daily newspapers. The 'transfigured self' of the seriously ill is more like a 'disfigurement', because I have become not more than myself but less than myself. That is why Transfiguration, if it is to mean anything, must point to the cross, to the disfigurement of Jesus on Calvary. In the same sermon (a Lenten preaching, not delivered for the August festival, which was at Rome some centuries away), we hear from Leo the words, 'amid the trials of life we should rather pray for endurance than glory because the joy of reigning cannot anticipate temporal suffering.'[5] Glory and suffering belong together, and that applies as much to the hospital patient, with their own vulnerability that they had probably only known there and then for the first time in their lives, as to any other struggling follower of Christ.

When it comes to the three narratives, the three portraits provided by Mark, Matthew and Luke show, once more, significant differences, which this time give no impression of being tucked away in the sidelines. All that they seem to have in common is that Jesus' clothing became 'dazzling white'. From there, everything seems up for grabs. Mark describes the clothes as so white that 'no one on earth could bleach them'; Matthew says that his face 'shone like the sun', whereas Mark makes no mention of his face at all; and whereas both Mark and Matthew describe the process as being 'transfigured' ('metamorphosed'), Luke uses a more roundabout term, 'the appearance of his face changed', adding beforehand 'and while he was praying', as if to reinforce the previous verse (Luke 9:28), where he says that Jesus took the three up the mountain 'to pray'.

These cannot be mere casual variants, as if we were comparing three portrayals of Queen Elizabeth II, whether in royal robes, military uniform, or sitting by the fireside; or three icons, which, even though painted according to the conventions, nonetheless give us different postures for the disciples, different physical relationships between Jesus and the two Old Testament figures, and with only one of them including the small vignettes of the ascent and descent of the mountain; nor yet of three portrayals of a hospital patient undergoing treatment for a life-threatening illness. They need to be seen in the whole context of each gospel.

While both Mark and Matthew use the expression 'was transfigured', the implication being that God did the transfiguring, Mark's version comes over with more subtlety, almost ambiguity. Well, was it really God who transfigured? No mention is made of Jesus' face, suggesting a dimension of unknowability. And yet he goes to town on those clothes, which only a few chapters earlier were the source of healing (Mark 5:27–31) for the woman who had suffered from haemorrhages for twelve years. Here, that same clothing – we are led to believe – radiates a degree of whiteness that is out of this world. All in all, it is a heavenly and not an earthly event. Heil sums it up as follows: 'it is a physical transformation of his external appearance visible in his clothing.'[6] And he draws attention to the sharpness of the Greek words 'radiating' (*stilbonta*) the 'extreme' (*lian*) whiteness of the garment. A bleacher is someone who cleans woollen cloth, although the verb 'radiating' is used in the Septuagint (the Greek version of the Old Testament) for the gleaming of polished brass (1 Esd. 8:56; 2 Esd. 8:27), or steel (Nahum 3:3), or sunlight (1 Macc. 6:39).[7]

Overall, too, the ambiguity comes across in the implication – and it is only an implication – that the scene involved glory. Yet glory is not mentioned, even though it is Mark who refers to the coming of the Son of Man in glory (Mark 8:38). Dorothy Lee even goes as far as to say that Mark's inner, tantalising ambiguity (my words, not hers) suggests that it is even left open as to whether such a glory came from within Jesus, or from God.[8] Could it be that Mark's non-mention of Jesus' face is supposed to be covered by the mention of the clothing? Or (more likely) is Mark deliberately talking up the clothing to draw attention to his desire to play down the face? All in all, even though Mark's is not the most preached-upon gospel narrative, and even though preachers down the ages have often referred in passing to his reference to the heavenly bleacher, what he produces overall is unique, and when we observe his special features closely, we can only lament the traditional almost exclusive concentration on Matthew's version.

But Matthew's version has its own features as well. With the mountain symbolism in his gospel so deeply embedded, there is more of a theological association with the unknown venue up there. Here is where divine action takes place, as with Moses, whose face shone on Mount Sinai (Exod. 34:29–35). As Lee observes, 'the radiance of Jesus' face parallels the radiance of Moses giving the Law.'[9] And whereas Mark speaks of clothing that is whiter than anything earth can manage, Matthew speaks of Jesus' face shining like the sun. For him, such cosmic touches are not coincidental. The magi followed a star from the east (Matt. 2:1); at the moment of Jesus' death, when the temple curtain was torn in two, 'the earth shook, and the rocks were split. The tombs were opened, and many bodies of the saints who had fallen asleep were raised' (Matt. 27:51–52).

One could go further still, and point to the significance of light in the teaching of Jesus (Matt. 5:14–16; 6:22–23; 10:27). Lee summarises this point of view: 'the light shines out of surrounding darkness, illuminating the inner being as well as the outer world.' Perhaps this theme of light can be pushed even further, as a few chapters earlier, Matthew's Jesus has been teaching about the righteous at the day of judgement shining like the sun in the kingdom of the Father (Matt. 13:43). This kind of parallelism brings out a different kind of subtlety from Mark, in all his brevity: here Transfiguration comes across to the audience, the worshipper gazing at the icon, as an anticipation of future glory. As Heil remarks, Jesus' clothing 'has now attained the extreme whiteness characteristic of the clothing of those who dwell in heaven'.[10] All in all, Matthew's narrative draws together the themes of future judgement and future glory in equal measure. And we shall hear more of how the 'uncreated light' is dealt with when we look at the fourteenth-century Greek writer, Gregory Palamas (Chapter 7).

Luke, as we have noted before, seems deliberately to avoid the word 'metamorphosed', and prefers the much more naturalistic expression, 'the appearance of his face changed'. But that is juxtaposed to the (repeated) context of prayer, and although (as we have also already observed) Luke likes to place important events in Jesus' life in the context of prayer, of all those events which the Transfiguration most resembles, it is the baptism of Jesus. For whereas Luke – uniquely – describes the Spirit descending on Jesus at his baptism 'in bodily form' (*eidei* – Luke 3:22), so here his appearance (*eidos*) went through a change.[11] The root for *eidos* in Greek is about seeing; the word is related to the Latin *video*, meaning 'I see', as in 'vision'. So it would not be stretching the imagination to conclude that behind and beneath Luke's words both at the baptism and at Transfiguration are the onlookers' perceptions: the Spirit seen like a body, and Jesus seen as changed, with a very strong word for 'dazzling', the same used of the angels at the empty tomb (Luke 24:4). In some ways, this carries even more weight than the (religiously more conventional) term 'metamorphosed', with its overtones of Hellenistic Greek religion, which Luke, as someone steeped in that background, would want to avoid.

What comes across from Luke's account is a slightly different way from Mark's and Matthew's of expressing both the temporary, but real, character of the Transfiguration. Jesus enters into glory, a word which he uses twice later in his narrative, and which does not appear explicitly in either of the other two (Luke 9:31–32). And the advantage with Luke is that we have Acts as a further point of comparison. When Stephen was arraigned before the Jewish council, 'they saw that his face was like that of an angel' (Acts 6:15). The same word for 'dazzling' is used of the light that flashes at Paul on the road to Damascus (Acts 9:3; 23:6). Luke's mannerisms are frequently mentioned in sermons on the Matthew narrative, because preachers saw their importance. But, of course, one only really senses the character of each narrative by reflecting specifically on them. For Luke, the language of Transfiguration combines the earthly, in the words he used to describe the event itself, and the heavenly, in the piercing light that emanates, albeit temporarily from Christ himself.

Jesus' clothing has fascinated interpreters down the ages. As we shall see later on (Chapter 9), Origen is really the father of the allegorical interpretation of the New Testament. For him, Jesus' garments are the gospel, whereas Ambrose, at the end of the fourth century, took them to mean the Scriptures as a whole, and Augustine, later on still, regarded them as representing the Church.[12] These are not clever fancies to be set aside by an apparently more sophisticated audience of today. The question must be asked: what motivated such brilliant expositors as Origen, preaching in Palestine in the first part of the third century, Ambrose in Milan in the next, and Augustine in Hippo not much later than that, to take such views? The answer lies in the need to place the Scriptures in the possession of the whole Church, as living words that for all their diversity have a unity, found in Christ alone, words that require imaginative interpretation, inspired by the Spirit. A yet more ecclesiological interpretation of Christ's clothing is linked to baptism, the sacrament where we make our entry, our covenant with the Redeemer himself. Several medieval Western writers connect Christ's clothing with the teaching of St Paul: 'as many of you as were baptized by Christ have clothed yourselves with Christ' (Gal. 3:27). These start with Bede (c. 673–735), who is followed by others including Anselm, Archbishop of Canterbury (d. 1109), and Peter of Blois, Archdeacon of Bath (d. 1204).[13] It is something of an irony that at precisely the time when it might be said that the Western Church was beginning to lose its grip on baptism as *the* sacrament which expresses the nature of the Church, we encounter three quite different writers who made the important connection between the Jordan and Tabor – not just for Jesus, but for all of us.

That garment is, therefore, a main point of contact. It perhaps explains why in icons of the Transfiguration his clothing is dazzling white, whereas his body does not actually look all that different from how he is depicted in other scenes of his life. It is as if the 'new form' that his body takes on is so different that it is impossible to portray, whereas one of the consequences of that change is the shining garment. On that score, the intention of each gospel-writer is to show how we become part of the scene ourselves – and that makes us yet again both the audience of the drama and the transformed worshipper.

Transfiguration is a big notion and, as we have discovered in other ways so far, one of the issues that the Christian Church has struggled with is how to fit it in with the yearly round of major feasts (Christmas and Easter), with their times of preparation (Advent and Lent), their extensions onwards (Epiphany and Ascension–Pentecost), as well as the 'green season', sometimes nowadays called 'Ordinary Time'. At the Danish Reformation, a practical solution was found. The inheritance was to read the narrative in the traditional patristic way on the Saturday before the Second Sunday in Lent, and also to observe the (comparatively new) feast on 6 August. The (even newer) custom at Rome of reading it on the Second Sunday in Lent itself had not been adopted in Northern Europe, where the older gospel reading remained, the Canaanite woman coming to Jesus and arguing with him to heal her daughter (Matt. 15:21–28). Since the calendar feast days were being reduced drastically anyway, and other Lutheran reforms elsewhere had abolished the commemoration of the Transfiguration on 6 August, it seemed a pity to get rid of a reading that was so central to the life of Jesus. So an ingenious solution was found: have the Matthew narrative, together with the Transfiguration epistle (2 Pet. 1:12–18), on the Sunday in the year for which there was no provision. This is the 'extra' Sunday which every so often crops up because of the vagaries of the yearly cycle, either at the end of the Trinity season (the twenty-seventh Sunday) or the Epiphany season (the sixth Sunday).

This has resulted in a significant drip-feed process of Transfiguration into the Danish Lutheran tradition. And in Denmark, the clearest signal, apart from preaching, is the writing of hymns, where so much of its liturgical theology is to be located. In the seventeenth century, Thomas Kingo (1634–1703), Bishop of Odense, was responsible for writing an official hymnbook in 1699, but the composition by him before the sermon for this occasion, while full of rich language, is a meditation on the Kingdom of God rather than specifically on the Transfiguration.[14] Yet its whole tenor would nonetheless suggest to the preacher an eschatological note. Exactly such a note is struck, but with far greater focus on the Transfiguration itself, in the preaching and hymn-writing of someone who made a very considerable contribution to Danish church life two centuries on – Nikolai Grundtvig (1783–1872).[15]

Grundtvig was the son of a pastor who after a brilliant but at times stormy time was ordained in 1811. An unusual and creative personality, he was also difficult to label in the overall spectrum of theology at the time. He was part traditionalist, part romantic, part modern. He rejected any rationalistic reduction of the liturgy, for example, when the works of the devil are renounced at baptism. Appointed pastor at Præstø in 1821, in the following year he was made an assistant pastor at the Church of our Saviour (Vor Frelsers Kirke) in Copenhagen, but he resigned after further controversies in 1826. He visited England three times between 1829 and 1831 in order to study Norse mythology. After a time as honorary curate at the Christianskirke in Copenhagen, the right job was found for him, at Vartov Hospital in 1839, where he remained as a regular preacher, unencumbered by parish concerns, until his death. His poetic genius bore fruit in a vast outpouring of hymns, four hundred in 1837, many of them reworkings of older hymns, not just from the Danish Reformation, but from medieval Latin and from Greek sources, a less than usual source for hymnwriters of his tradition at the time. In all he wrote over fifteen hundred hymns, and while it took time for them to be generally accepted, his is the single most frequent name attached to the hymns of the Danish Church today.

From Grundtvig we have no fewer than three sermons and five hymns on the Transfiguration – which places him far ahead of any other writer we have so far encountered, with the exception of Hacket's course of seven sermons. The three sermons were delivered in the Holmenskirke (the Navy Church) in Copenhagen on 11 February 1821; in the Christianskirke on 26 November 1837; and in Vartov on 25 November 1845.[16] His five hymns date from 1837 (a lengthy exposition), three in 1853 (the first, in short four-line verses is the best known), and a final hymn from the later period, 1860–62.[17]

The Danish word for Transfiguration is *Forklarelse*, which means something to do with 'making clear', 'manifesting', and this permeates both the three sermons and the five hymns. With his poetic feel for words, Grundtvig knows how to use repetition in different contexts. But there are two other words that he repeats, *ansigt* (face), and *menighed* (congregation), though the latter probably corresponds to what some would more generally refer to as 'Church'. Christ's face appears in a 'clarified' form. But it is no past historical event. Grundtvig is more conscious than any other writer we have seen so far, or indeed those that we have yet to look at later on, of the gap in time between the original event on that mountain and the event as it is liturgically celebrated in the reading and preaching of the Word, as well as in the sacraments of baptism and eucharist. In the 1837 hymn, perhaps the richest of all, with no fewer than 15 verses of 9-line stanzas, but not sung today (probably because no suitable melody has emerged for the metre), he refers in the last verse to the two sacraments in an expression used elsewhere in his hymnody as *badet* and *bordet* – bath and board.

For Grundtvig's essentially liturgical theology, the *forklarelse* takes place in the *menighed* (the congregation), here and now, even though it is (for him) eighteen hundred years on. So concerned is he with the need for God to renew the Church that he even speaks of the *alderdom* (old age) of the Church, tired with history and tired with conflict. Indeed, the 1821 sermon, part of a collection of material reworked and expanded after delivery, is (significantly) placed at the head of the whole series, indicating the importance he attaches to a theme that was not part of every annual cycle of preaching-texts; near the start he openly admits the unfamiliar character of the narrative, as well as its overall strangeness to contemporary ears. He has, however, a supreme confidence in the eternal truths of the gospel to be proclaimed and lived, in spite of our fallen nature. And the focus is the liturgical celebration. As Hans Hemmingsen says of Grundtvig, in a context that is social, but that can just as easily apply to worship, 'Grundtvig himself was incapable of thinking individualistically.'[18] Even the candles lit on the altar convey for him something of this Christ-centred *forklarelse*. Rebelling against what he saw as the shallowness of pietism and the aridity of rationalism, he brings to the fore a gospel that engages with the whole personality, with its need for roots and tradition, and a hunger for a religion where both thinking and feeling together (and not kept apart) can help to form a mature faith. This is particularly striking in the 1853 hymn, when it speaks of the 'flashing-wreath' warming us 'right inside, to the very roots of our hearts.'

Another device Grundtvig uses is to relate the sermons with the time of the year. This means that whereas the February 1821 sermon looks forward to the cross, the November 1837 and 1845 sermons point towards the coming new church year, and Christmas after that. In the 1821 sermon, he sows the seed of God's purposes not being thwarted, whether it was after Christ's birth, with Herod's attempt to kill him, or with the martyrdom of Stephen – where his eyes were *forklaredes* (transfigured). The 1837 sermon, by contrast, links the Transfiguration with the ministry of John the Baptist, soon to be proclaimed in the ensuing Advent, with Christ's baptism thirty years later, another indication of Grundtvig's sense of time and eternity in history. And as for Origen, Ambrose and Augustine before him, the Scriptures are not there to remain dead letters, but the living Word, in Christ. Then there is the 1845 sermon, which ends on an even stronger eschatological note than is customary with Grundtvig, another suggestion of Advent being round the corner: in the *forklarelse* Jesus gives us a glimpse through the light, his face, his clothing, of the glory that is yet to come. God's *røst* (voice) calls, challenges, and effects salvation, even in the ambiguities and ambivalences of human nature: the Spirit can work on the *støvet* (dust) of human life. But the refreshing aspect of these sermons and hymns is that however rooted they are in a sense of a living tradition, with the liturgy as the focus, there is no ecclesiastical triumphalism. For Grundtvig, the awkward, creative poet-preacher, faith is not easy – but it is still a heavenly gift. And part of the process of struggling with the paradox of faith is what Donald Allchin describes as follows: 'his wonderful sense of the poetic, many-layered nature of language, his feeling for the living presence of the past, in and through the vicissitudes of history, point towards a church which is at one with its freely accepted diversity.'[19] For Grundtvig, therefore, Transfiguration is no feast, but an essential part of Christian discipleship.

Iconography is only one of the arts. Sculpture is another. Both of them give some clue to the question 'How?' that is posed by the change that Transfiguration, *forklarelse*, brings about, both in Christ and in ourselves. Above the altar in Copenhagen Cathedral stands a massive sculpted figure of Christ by Bertel Thorvaldsen (1770–1844), who was let loose on the new building after its predecessor was destroyed during the British bombardment in 1807. The 'Fruekirke' (Church of Our Lady) is a plain classical structure, with Thorvaldsen statues of the twelve apostles on either side in the nave. But it is the Christ-figure, placed there in 1837, who commands attention, standing there in white marble, with one foot slightly ahead of the other, and strongly welcoming hands. The biblical text carved above is from Matthew's Transfiguration narrative: 'this is my Son, the Beloved; with him I am well pleased; listen to him' (Matt. 17:5).

A statue makes a different kind of impact from a painting.

But in such a stark building, all these Thorvaldsen works of art are at home. There is even a large angel holding the baptismal font, placed in the centre of the chancel, as if itself bearing a close relation to the Christ-figure some feet away, a juxtaposition that would delight Christian Thodberg, who has spent many years working on Grundtvig's theology, and the centrality of baptism to his whole sense of Christian identity. It is Jesus who is at the heart of Transfiguration, and he beckons us to come to him in order to share in that transformation. The massive proportions of the statue do not make it overwhelming, because it is completely at home in the overall scale of the building. And because it is not a painting, colours do not come into it. Transfiguration is not indicated by dazzling clothes, but by the whole figure, garments and all, both heavenly and earthly, as Grundtvig's preaching and hymnody make so clear.

Whenever we 'read' Transfiguration – and in Denmark it will be only on those occasional Sundays before Lent or Advent – there is a dual background, of the coming Christ, in the heavenly Kingdom, and of the Christ who goes on to suffering and death. Some of this comes through together with the evocative image of 'the light of the knowledge of the glory of God in the face of Jesus Christ' (2 Cor. 4:6) in an introduction to Evening Prayer on Fridays and in Lent written by David Stancliffe:

> Blessed are you, Lord God of our salvation,
> To you be glory and praise for ever.
> In the darkness of our sin you have shone in our hearts
> To give the light of the knowledge of the glory of God
> In the face of Jesus Christ.
> As we behold your Son, enthroned on the cross,
> Stir up in us the fire of your love,
> That we may be cleansed from all our sins,
> And walk with you as children of light.
> Blessed be God, Father, Son and Holy Spirit.[20]

Chapter 5

VISITORS

He brings forward both him that died and him that never yet suffered.[1]

(John Chrysostom, c. 347–407)

And there appeared to them Elijah with Moses, who were talking with Jesus.

(Mark 9:4)

Suddenly there appeared to them Moses and Elijah talking to him.

(Matt. 17:3)

Suddenly they saw two men, Moses and Elijah, talking to him. They appeared in glory and were speaking of his departure, which he was about to accomplish at Jerusalem. Now Peter and his companions were weighed down with sleep, but since they had stayed awake, they saw his glory and the two men who stood with him.

(Luke 9:30–32)

Visitors can make or break an occasion. But the one thing they do manage to achieve is to change things on arrival. As I lay in hospital, I knew who the regular visitors were and when they were likely to come. There were the 'in-house' visitors, such as the nurse who came in shortly after 6.00 a.m. for the first of the small daily checkups. Then there was the daily visit from the doctor, whether it was one of the younger ones, or one of the consultants. And it could be one of the auxiliaries coming in to clean my room. Nearer home, the visitors could be Sarah, my wife, arriving most days at 12 noon and staying until early evening. Hers were the visits that felt the most essential, providing a measure of support that no one else could. She also brought in her own kind of drip-feed – family and other gossip, and some post and even the odd e-mail, which was filtered through from the office. With leukaemia, it is important to have a life outside the illness. I was even told that a positive attitude can set the body up in such a way as to be more receptive to treatment. That meant, too, that visits from other members of the family, such as our children, were just as important. And because their visits were more inter-mittent, they had a different kind of impact.

Because of the acute nature of the illness, and the nature of the job I had, we kept all other outside visits down to an absolute minimum, even at the risk of causing offence. A very few colleagues were allowed in, but everyone else was kept at bay. At first this was common sense. In those first four weeks when I was in hospital without any break, I didn't really want to see anyone else. The routine settled, and the days began and continued and ended with the kind of daily round I've just described. Later on, of course, things did change, as I got stronger and stronger, and my spells at home became more and more frequent. So 'surprise' visitors began to appear. And it was these who made a different kind of impact. It was they who 'gate-crashed' a routine that had developed around me. A nurse would pop in and say, 'You've got so-and-so outside – do you want to see them?' Almost invariably I would agree. The surprise element altered the whole dynamic, and even more so if I had Sarah or someone else who came more frequently there beside me. Suddenly the focus would be on them, what they had to bring to the visit, especially if I had not seen them for some time. They became a different kind of link with the outside world, and with my past. And sometimes there might even be a kind of reconciliation element to the visit as well. Visitors *are*, but they also *talk*(!), and it's interesting to observe the people who know how to visit well, and those who can't.

In the case of the Transfiguration scene, it is Moses and Elijah, the visitors, who helped to define the whole event, for up to now it has been an 'in-house' experience of Jesus with the three disciples, Peter, James and John. Up to now, they have had their mountain-trek and reached the summit, where the appearance of Jesus changes. But whatever the nature of that change, it is what happens after that has taken place that expresses what it means, whether we are talking about Moses and Elijah's arrival and their interaction with Jesus, or Peter's impulsive response, or the descent of the cloud, or the voice, or the disciples' response to all that, as they walk back down to everyday life. Moses and Elijah are the visitors who intrude on the scene. This, at any rate, is how their arrival comes across in the narrative, to the audience, to the worshipper gazing at the icon. Moses and Elijah, central figures to Israel's past, and, as we shall see, figures who therefore keep reappearing in sacred discourse, turn that mountain-top scene into something which is definitely – and no longer just probably – extraordinary. They may belong to the category of figures whom Jesus and the disciples discussed from time to time, but they are no longer alive. They are *representative* figures from the religious inheritance. They are not routine, day-to-day people who were part and parcel of the daily experience of Jesus with his followers. Their visit helps to define this Transfiguration and they help the disciples, the audience, the onlookers, to understand its meaning – over and above a walk with Jesus at the end of which he suddenly (and temporarily) looks different.

Eastern iconography handles them with due care, though not always in exactly the same way. Theophanes the Greek depicts Christ at the centre of a circular 'mandorla' at the summit of Tabor, with rays going down to the three disciples at the foot. A unique feature is the innovation of two huge vector-like shapes behind Christ, which express the twofold character of the Transfiguration – descent and ascent. When it comes to the two visitors, Moses on the right and Elijah on the left stand on what look like separate mountains; they are outside the mandorla and there are no rays from Jesus reaching them.[2] Other icons employ an oval mandorla, which Andreopoulos sees as representing the luminance of God, a prime example of which is the mosaic at St Catherine's, on Mount Sinai, and it has rays coming from Christ that reach Moses and Elijah as well as the disciples. The circular mandorla Andreopoulos interprets as expressing the accessible glory of God, a tabernacle rather than a luminance, a prime example of which is the sixteenth-century icon in the monastery of Pantokrator on Mount Athos, a good century after Theophanes the Greek's icon; and it has the same overall shape, complete with the vignettes of Jesus leading the disciples and then leading them down.

Close theological interpretations of details of iconography, even of Eastern iconography, could run the risk of splitting hairs. But Andreopoulos' study repays careful attention. What is important for our purposes in looking at Moses and Elijah is how they are depicted. They have to be there, because of their defining role, in portraying Transfiguration as something that involves heavenly beings. And their relationship with Jesus is of importance. The two shapes of mandorla surrounding Christ come across differently. Circularity is more inclusive than an oval shape. A circle surrounds Jesus but we are led into him, whereas an oval shape delineates in a more exclusive way. Both are right, and neither is wrong. But the circular shape perhaps tips the balance in the direction of accessibility at a time when, in the Greek tradition (as we shall see later, in Chapter 7), there was a need to emphasise that Transfiguration was a mystery that was not just for some, but for everyone. Similarly, those separate 'mountainettes' on which Moses and Elijah stand at first sight may baffle, but they are perhaps there in order to demonstrate their subordinate nature. As Andreopoulos goes on to suggest, 'the three parts of Tabor show that Moses, Elijah, and Christ each had a different mountain to climb and different tasks to perform.'[3] Rays that reach them draw them into the scene. Rays that bring only the disciples into the scene show that Transfiguration is to draw the audience, the worshipper, the disciples, into this new disclosure of salvation. And if the rays are mathematically drawn from an oval mandorla, as in the case of the miniature mosaic made in Constantinople, *c.* 1200, then the impact is both exclusive in relation to Christ and also cosmic – the Lord not only of time but of space as well.[4]

So much for visitors and the conventions of iconography. The question nonetheless remains, 'How were they recognised?' Visitors to my hospital bed were always familiar, because they were people I knew. Religious art has a habit of building up its own momentum, through the conventions that surround particular events. A Transfiguration icon has Jesus on a mountain, and if there is any doubt as to whether this is in fact the scene, there are always three terror-struck disciples and the two Old Testament figures on either side. In an age that knew no television, and had no proper archives of traditional likenesses, how could Peter, James and John know who Jesus was talking to? In his *Harmony of the Evangelists*, a carefully crafted commentary-in-one on the four Gospels, John Calvin (1509–64) asks exactly this question, and he provides the reply: 'God, who brought them forward, gave also signs and tokens by which they were enabled to know them.'[5] One can only guess that the conversation – as is the case of all visitors – gave away their identity, and (more important) their relationship to Jesus.

The arrival of these visitors is recorded with remarkable divergences by the evangelists. Whereas Matthew and Luke put Moses before Elijah, Mark has 'Elijah with Moses', and Mark and Luke both begin with 'behold', often translated as 'suddenly', in order to draw attention to an unusual happening. And Mark specifies that the two are talking with Jesus. We shall come back to some of these variations shortly. But the most idiosyncratic account is given by Luke, who first describes the two visitors as 'two men', as if making clear that something both unusual and real is taking place. He also includes an additional sentence, which provides two significant points of context: they are 'in glory', with Jesus, and therefore not in the same level as the three disciples, and the conversation is specifically about Jesus' 'departure' ('exodus') that is to take place in Jerusalem. Luke also adds the reference to the disciples being 'weighed down with sleep', implying that this took place at night, when Jesus often prayed (Luke 6:12). Luke, the most historically minded of the evangelists, is keen to make the Transfiguration lead on to the next main event in the chronology of Jesus' life. This Lucan addition is constantly referred to by preachers down the centuries, even though the liturgical text is the Matthew narrative. It is too important to miss. All three narratives, however, make clear that the Transfiguration is an event that takes place for them: 'there appeared *to them*' in Mark and Matthew, contrasting with the gentler but still emphatic '*they saw*' in Luke. The Transfiguration is something that Jesus experiences, but it is an event with an audience, an icon with worshippers. As Swete notes, 'the vision is for the benefit of the disciples.'[6]

What, then, of these variants? Mark's apparent priority of Elijah could, in fact, be interpreted in both ways. Heil considers his use of 'with' as a way of making the opposite point, that it means 'not only Elijah but even Moses', whereas Lee considers Mark placing Elijah ahead of Moses because of expectations at the time of Elijah returning (cf. Mal. 4:5).[7] There is much to said for drawing out Mark's constant use of Elijah: right at the start, John the Baptist, the opening figure in the gospel, is seen as a prophetic figure fulfilling the promise of 'sending a messenger' before the people (Mal. 1:2–3). And Mark's Jesus, like both Elijah and John the Baptist, goes on to suffer not only persecution but rejection. Whether we take this view or not, however, it is Mark who 'talks up' both Moses and Elijah. Moses represents the Law (Mark 1:44) and gives the commandments of God (Mark 7:9–10), whereas Elijah is someone of such significance that Jesus is confused with him as a wonder-worker (Mark 6:15; 8:28). And here they are, both of them, in conversation with Jesus.

For Matthew, Elijah is not as important as Moses, the teacher of the Law. Matthew is the evangelist who brings Egypt, the place from which the people of Israel fled oppression, into the birth-narrative (Matt. 2:1–18); and we have already seen how central the symbolism of mountains is to this gospel (Chapter 3), supremely in the Sermon on the Mount (Matt. 5—7). For Matthew, Jesus is the new Moses, not providing a new Law, but bringing its true and inner meaning to light (Matt. 3:15). Moses and Elijah, therefore, appear at the Transfiguration as essential background, but they do not share the light of Christ, except in so far as their light is derived from him. Both of them paid dearly for their way of obeying the call of God, Moses dying of old age (Deut. 34:10), Elijah being taken up into heaven in a chariot (2 Kings 2:11). As we shall see shortly, much is made of this by John Chrysostom. According to Matthew, John the Baptist is the Elijah who was to come (Matt. 11:14), even though some likened Jesus to him (Matt. 16:14). All this serves to emphasise Matthew's focus on the identity and role of Jesus.

When we come to Luke, the contrast with the other two is greater still. Lee may be right in comparing the 'two men' description of Moses and Elijah with the two angels at the resurrection (Luke 24:4; Acts 1:10). Luke has already referred to Moses as the giver of the Law at the Presentation in the Temple (Luke 2:22), and at the healing of the leper (Luke 5:14). Elijah has been described as a 'prophetic reformer' (Luke 1:17) and a 'wonder-worker' (Luke 4:25–26) – and some people think that he has come back to life in Jesus, earlier in the same chapter in which the Transfiguration is recounted (Luke 9:8, 19). Luke's theme of glory brings out the heavenly character of the Transfiguration. In his gospel heavenly glory is already an established motif: an angel appears to Zechariah, the father of John the Baptist (Luke 1:11), and the angels sing of glory in heaven at Christ's birth (Luke 2:14). Moreover, Jesus has just told the disciples of the Son of Man coming in glory (Luke 9:26).

All this adds up to a definite picture of heavenly figures, something of a quite different order from the positioning of the three disciples on the mountain-top. The heavenly context of where these figures are then moves on to the specific context of their conversation with Jesus: what is going to happen to him next in his earthly life. And the point here is the sheer uniqueness of Jesus' death. Unlike the two Old Testament figures, for all their centrality to Israel's past and present, Jesus is going to be put to death, not just anywhere, but in Jerusalem. His 'departure' is of a quite different order from theirs. He is to be rejected (Luke 9:22), and his death does not just happen, it is 'accomplished', which implies that this is God's purpose. It is how things have to happen, as the risen Christ explains to the two disciples on the way to Emmaus (Luke 24:26). But then Luke introduces his own note of artistry. The disciples are there, but then they begin to awake. This suggests that they did not overhear the conversation, which would help to explain their obtuseness when Jesus did die and rise again. They don't witness the Transfiguration, nor do they witness the appearance of Moses and Elijah. But they wake up to the consequences.

71

But why Moses and Elijah? Ever since the time of Origen, whose treatment of the Transfiguration we shall be looking at later (Chapter 9), there has been a tendency to divide them up, sometimes quite rigidly, into the Law and the Prophets.[8] Calvin softens this line, allowing Elijah to be seen as a representative of the prophets, but makes his preference clear that 'Law and Prophets' do not imply for him two entirely separate compartments.[9] Lee, however, challenges this view, on the grounds that Moses 'is not just the giver of the law but the greatest of the prophets', and she goes on to suggest that Elijah was just as much a champion of the right observance of the law as he was a prophet.[10] Neat distinctions are not always helpful, and Lee probably has a point. It is perhaps more in the way we understand Jesus that Moses and Elijah in their complementary roles come across: together they represent the faith in which Jesus was nurtured, with its tradition and its inbuilt critique of religious faith and practice, which over time come to be associated with the two 'arms' of Judaism. Both the Law and the Prophets are challenged and fulfilled – together and in one person – through the life and death of Jesus of Nazareth. As Plummer noted some time ago, 'the three apostles saw the forms of two men *who were such as to be* recognized as Moses and Elijah, – the representatives of the Law and the Prophets. The power to recognize them was granted with the power to see them; otherwise the sight would have been meaningless.'[11]

Moses and Elijah provide a context for the Transfiguration which makes it what it is. They push the event into other realms. It is more than just Jesus looking different. It is about that knife-edge that runs right through the gospels – the tension between continuity and discontinuity. Up to now, they were both the past and, to some extent, the present. Every devout Jew, Jesus and the three disciples included, looked on them as formative figures, representing Israel's struggle to express and to live their faith in community. But now that is to be changed. They stand there as 'sponsors' for

Jesus, in Luke's terms, with him in glory, because Jesus both fulfils and subsumes the Law and the Prophets in his own person and work. The balance between continuity and dis-continuity is sometimes one of the most difficult aspects of faith, because it is about building on the past, knowing it and cherishing it better, in order to move into a future which is unknown because it is the future and not the past.

That is probably why Luke provides more detail about this particular episode in the Transfiguration: why are the visitors there? Because they stand in relation to Jesus about his future, a future different from theirs, because it involves far more than they ever suffered – being put to death as part of the purposes of God. All three evangelists tell of their appearance, and the fact that they are speaking with Jesus. A conversation implies a relationship, a duality. It was clearly not just Jesus who was doing the talking! But a conversation also implies growing understanding – something in which the disciples, whoever they are, including the audience of the here and now, are supposed to grow in. And because understanding the meaning of Jesus is not a once-for-all event in any person's life, that audience keeps returning to the same events in the Saviour's life.

It is impossible to take in the reception-history of the Transfiguration without looking at the preaching of John Chrysostom (c. 347–407), who gained his nickname 'golden-mouthed' because of his reputation in that area. The sermon in question, which gained a prominent position in Eastern tradition after the festival was established, comes from a series of ninety sermons on Matthew's Gospel. It dates from 390, when John was a presbyter in Antioch, the time in his life when his reputation for exegetical preaching was gaining prominence. It was probably this characteristic that attracted attention, and led to his being made Patriarch of Con-stantinople in 398, his subsequent confrontation with the moral laxity of the imperial court, the hostility of his rival

Theophilus of Alexandria, and his eventual exile in 404.[12] These sermons have been described by Kelly as 'the earliest and most extensive patristic commentary on the first gospel'.[13] The style of his approach to Scripture is often described as 'Antiochene', in that it expounds the text in a literal and moral manner, without the allegorical trimmings associated with the 'Alexandrian' approach, which we shall see later on when we look at the preaching of Origen (Chapter 9).

The three most important aspects about Chrysostom's fifty-sixth homily in this series are that it is part of a series on the gospel, and therefore nothing to do with any feast; that it starts with the verse of promise that immediately precedes the narrative (Matt. 16:28); and that it has a lengthy moral ending, condemning injustice and financial shady dealing.[14] Sachot thinks that it was probably delivered during Lent as part of a course of sermons, and he has shown how subsequent collections of homilies edited out the beginning and the end of Chrysostom's original text, so that what was left consisted only of his treatment of Matthew 17:1–9, which would accord more with the purposes of using it as a source for preaching on the 6 August festival.[15] It was not just what he said that influenced later preaching, it was some of the details of the exegesis of the man often referred to as 'the golden-mouthed' theologian in the East that make his work so important.

Chrysostom begins by referring back to the preceding verses, the prediction of the passion, which was how the previous sermon ended, and applies this to the immediate, practical context – we should not 'grieve any more, either over [our] own death, or over that of [our] Lord.' The disciples – we – continue to be taught by Jesus: 'he leads them on the gentler way.' Those who will 'see the Son of Man coming in his Kingdom' have nothing to fear, because this is a promise of hope. He then applies this to the three, as 'leaders' among the apostles, Peter because of his love for Jesus, John for being loved by him, and James because of his martyrdom; only these three, because the others would have wanted to be there, had they known what it would involve. But these three were chosen because they were 'readier to seize the high meaning' and so would 'be present with their mind quite awake and full of care'. This explanation is used frequently afterwards in the East. Two examples will suffice from the time after the festival was established: John of Damascus in the first half of the eighth century, and a much lesser-known figure, Philagathos of Cerami, a twelfth-century monk who compiled a large collection of sermons from his preaching ministry in Greek-speaking communities in Calabria; he preached on the Transfiguration in Rossano Cathedral.[16]

But why, then, Moses and Elijah? No fewer than five reasons are provided. First, because some said that Jesus was Elijah (Matt. 16:14), and Peter was rightly commended for confessing Jesus as the messiah. Second, because Jesus did not break the Law, one of the charges levelled against him (e.g. John 9:16; 10:33), but cared for the Law given by Moses. Third, because Elijah 'was jealous for the glory of God', and would have opposed anyone opposed to God. Moses and Elijah are thus established as allies of Jesus. Fourth, Jesus has power over life and death, so 'he brings forward both him that had died [i.e., Moses] and him that never suffered this [i.e., Elijah]'. These reasons keep recurring in later preaching, particularly the last one, with its clear distinction between the two figures, and the way it sets Jesus above them; among those who use this exegesis are Basil of Seleucia (d. *c.* 468), who also differentiates between Moses, the 'teacher of virtue' and Elijah 'fired with divine zeal'.[17] The fifth reason Chrysostom offers builds on the preceding ones, 'to show the glory of the cross, and to console Peter and the others in their dread of the passion, and to raise up their minds'.

This is the reason which makes Christ unique, as Chrysostom goes on to explain: Moses may have stood by to watch the sea part before the people of Israel, and Elijah may have raised a dead man, but that is nothing compared with what Jesus has done and is about to do. 'He brought [Moses and

Elijah] into glory too not that they should stay where they were but that they might even surpass their limits.' Transfiguration is about moving on – it is not about standing still. And that applies to all those involved, not just to the disciples, who are now witnesses, no longer only hearers, but to those who have gone before and those who are yet to be. Neither Moses nor Elijah are to be condemned, says Chrysostom. The Old Testament matters, and is not to be discarded – a message that comes from the heart of a dedicated expositor of both parts of the Christian Bible. 'To train them [i.e., the disciples] for all this, he brought forward those who shone forth under the old law.'

This is probably the most extensive treatment of the presence of Moses and Elijah in the early centuries. For John Chrysostom, who needs no allegory in order to get his message across, everything points to Christ, everything makes sense in the words and deeds of Jesus. He is not Moses, but he is no law-breaker. Elijah would have applauded his zeal for the glory of God. He indeed has the power over life and death, and can therefore descend in order to bring forward Moses and he can ascend in order to bring forward Elijah. And the purpose of this mountain-top experience is to teach the disciples about his coming death, its inevitability, its meaning, for all its awfulness, and the fact that in spite of everything, this is the way of God. Jesus is destined to go to places no one else has been before – not even the great figures of Israel's sacred past. At moments of crisis, it is natural, understandable, almost inevitable, that human beings look to familiar points of reference. What is happening to Jesus there? What would Moses and Elijah make of it? What would *they* say were they here? But they are here, and they are taking not front-row places, but they are standing aside, they are being brought into this new picture of how things are to be, and they seem to be approving.

The rest of Chrysostom's sermon deals with the ensuing events. Peter can't remain where Moses entered thick darkness and Elijah brought fire on the mountain. But he cannot understand the full meaning of what has happened: 'the exceeding greatness of the light weighed down the infirmity of their eyes.' The cloud that surrounds Jesus is bright, which expresses clarity and illumination, unlike the dark cloud that enveloped Moses, which expressed unclarity and mystery (Exod. 20:21; 19:18). 'He himself speaks nothing.' It is only the Father that speaks, harking back to the baptism at the river Jordan; the Son is 'equal to him in all respects', for 'there is but one will in him and in the Father.' But whereas at the baptism there was a crowd, here there is 'solitude, and height, and great quietness' – the Greek word for which is *hēsuchia,* which (as we shall see in Chapter 7) gave rise to a powerful monastic spirituality, hesychasm. Chrysostom moves straight on to Jesus telling them not to be afraid, for what they have just seen points forward to what is to come, the scandal of the cross. He ends by drawing his hearers into the promise of Transfiguration by speaking of the end of all things: 'we shall then behold Christ, not as they then on the mount, but in far greater brightness.' Then he exhorts them to 'lay aside our filthy garments' in order to live lives worthy of Christ's Transfiguration; and he rails against the sins of the people, financial included.

John Chrysostom's influence on subsequent Eastern writers was, as we have already noted, considerable. His pre-occupation with Moses and Elijah is reflected in the commentary on Matthew written by Ishod'ad of Merv (*c.* 850), of the so-called Nestorian Church (more properly called 'the Church of the East'), who was Bishop of Hedatta, on the River Tigris, in modern-day Iraq.[18] His concern with the divinity of the Transfiguration of Christ is developed by the author of a sermon that was for long attributed to Ephrem the Syrian (*c.* 306–73), but has since been identified as the work of two other Antiochene preachers, either Ephrem of Amid (Patriarch of Antioch, 527–45) or Isaac of Antioch (d. 460/461).[19] The latter part of this sermon, an extended meditation on the

Transfiguration, contrasts the human and the divine that coexist in Christ, and how these two natures can be seen in the different events in his life: 'if he was not in the flesh, who wore human garments? And if he was not God, who did acts of power and wonders?' Jesus is far more than Moses or Elijah, as the language about his two natures – reflecting the controversies of the fifth century – makes clear.

John Chrysostom was indeed a golden-mouthed preacher. But as we saw earlier (Chapter 4), Nikolai Grundtvig was a golden-mouthed hymn-writer, and it is not without significance that his lengthy 1837 hymn opens with the words, 'Jesus, Moses and Elijah, manifest in the cloud tent, / spoke highly about what the Messiah would endure, and bear on the cross.'[20] In all his hymns, it is the appearance of the two visitors that for him makes the Transfiguration what it is, a past event that is real now. For him, for Chrysostom, for many other preachers, the two figures represent the past, only in order to point to the uniqueness of Jesus, as the audience, the worshipper, is drawn into the movement that is depicted on the icon, and that is played out in the drama before us. If the question posed by Jesus' change of appearance is 'how?', then the question raised by this particular scene is 'with whom?'; and the answer must be familiar representative figures, vital at a time of uncertainty and tension about the future. The disciples needed points of reference for Jesus, if only as a means of comparison, but they can't depend on them in the same way any longer.

This is true also of anyone struggling to make sense of their faith. Soon after the diagnosis of my illness, I lay in my hospital getting used to the prospect of some time away from work. There were many thoughts that passed through my mind in those early days. What helped me feel secure was the confidence given by the professional care of doctors and nurses, and visits from my family and close colleagues. But there was one experience that I shall not forget which is hard to put into words. Early one evening, after Sarah had left, I was staring up at the ceiling in the corner of my room, directly ahead of me. For a few moments, I could see the faces of some of my forebears, likenesses of whom I had at home, stretching back over two centuries. They were not – quite yet! – welcoming me aboard: they were cheering me on. And then they were gone. In retrospect, of course, this 'waking dream' can be dismissed as the product of my unconscious, brought on by my state of mind, and helped by the effects of the drugs being pumped into me. But it was real, and it was a crucial part of the coping mechanisms – *in faith* – at that stage. Whatever I was to go through, and there was still a huge amount of that, that special moment of encouragement that seemed to say 'Go for it!', is something I shall never forget. There were no special colours, nor any music, except perhaps the odd Danish hymn that went through my mind afterwards. But it was a kind of 'mini-transfiguration', with my own personal Moses and Elijah equivalents. I was made ready for a journey that was yet to unfold.

There are many prayers that put this kind of personal journey into words, prayers that accept the past for what it is, but look forward to the future as a real challenge. In the Church of England *Book of Common Worship* (2000), the Collect for the 18th Sunday after Trinity dwells on precisely these themes, with a confidence, too, in the fact that God has 'commandments' in whose way we have yet to 'run'. As this scene of Old Testament 'visitors' makes plain, Jesus comes not to abolish the past, Israel's Law and Prophets, and all, but to fulfil and develop them. Paul's words to the Philippians spring to mind: 'I press on toward the goal for the prize of the heavenly call of God in Christ Jesus' (Phil. 3:14):

> Almighty and everlasting God,
> increase in us your gift of faith
> that, forsaking what lies behind
> and reaching out to that which is before,

we may run the way of your commandments
and win the crown of everlasting joy;
through Jesus Christ your Son our Lord,
who is alive and reigns with you,
in the unity of the Holy Spirit,
one God, now and for ever.[21]

Chapter 6

ENTHUSIASM

The Transfiguration will not always last.
(Mark Frank, 1613–64)[1]

Then Peter said to Jesus, 'Rabbi, it is good for us to be here, let us make three dwellings, one for you, one for Moses, and one for Elijah.' He did not know what to say, for they were terrified.
(Mark 9:5–6)

Then Peter said to Jesus, 'Lord, it is good for us to be here, if you wish, I will make three dwellings here, one for you, one for Moses, and one for Elijah.'
(Matt. 17:4)

Just as they were leaving him, Peter said to Jesus, 'Master, it is good for us to be here, let us make three dwellings, one for you, one for Moses, and one for Elijah' – not knowing what he said.
(Luke 9:33)

We now come to the one episode which is not enacted in the Transfiguration drama. Peter wants to build monuments of some kind to the event that has just happened. Every other episode can be read into the icon. The theme of promise is there from the start. The ascent of Jesus with the disciples is depicted on the left side of the mountain-complex in the icon of Theophanes the Greek, just as the descent is depicted on the other side. The change in Jesus is strong and bold, just as the cloud is there, and the voice of the Father in the background. It is all of a piece – except this sudden enthusiasm of Peter.

One of the most natural instincts in life is the desire to 'hold' a special event and keep it there. Photography is a modern development that captures scenes sometimes vividly. I have photographs that bring back not just loved ones who are no longer alive but events and experiences which the colour images express in ways that rekindle the memory. People use photography and video cameras in order to have a record of what happened. Sometimes this kind of equipment can get in the way – when I was a parish priest I used to keep the photographers on a tight rein at weddings, because they could easily become obtrusive. But they nonetheless provide a record of experiences which those close to the events can somehow re-live by pondering them. And the most treasured achieve – as the saying goes – 'iconic status'.

But can we really 'hold' events? Can we really halt history? Of course the answer is emphatically 'no'. But the desire to do so keeps recurring. When I am at my busiest there is part of me that resents the needful (and sometimes all too rapid) transition to the next thing to do. I want to be able to savour what has happened. I want to be on my own and think about it. At a public liturgy, I may have pronounced the dismissal, but inside there is a voice telling me that I really don't want to go to the church hall and join the melee of happy Christians in coffee-talk. I want to stay and ponder. I want to 'hold' the moment that meant so much, whether it was the disabled confirmation candidate, or the sick child who was anointed, or the devout farmer's rough hands at the altar-rail, or the hymn that summed it all up. These are my preferences, and they sometimes intrude. Peter's were different. He thought it was all over with the change in Jesus and the appearance of Moses and Elijah. And from the way in which he reacted – and it was an impulsive reaction, not a considered response – he did not understand what was happening, because he was putting Jesus on the same level as Moses and Elijah. We shall come back to the details of this reaction shortly. Meanwhile, it is worth pondering further what is really going on here.

Peter is speaking for stumbling faith that finds it hard to move onwards. Moses and Elijah represent familiarity, and their conversation with Jesus seems now to have little more significance than that it has taken place. If we add Luke's reference to the subject of their discussion – Jesus' 'departure' at Jerusalem – then it is almost as if it never really happened. Those tents, those shelters, those pieces of religious para-phernalia are about *confining* their presence in that specific moment, rather than providing a *focus* for them. Peter's enthusiasm is a very religious one! And herein lies the real crunch point, which draws the Transfiguration out of the confines of the mountain, and brings it right into the heart of religious experience: we are not speaking of a 'magic moment' that has somehow to be 'captured' for all time. For Christ's total silence, apart from his words to the disciples not to be afraid, only recounted by Matthew (Matt. 17:7), is the most eloquent aspect of the entire scene. We are, rather, con-templating a new way of God's presence with his people. It is not enough to think of Jesus as a teacher (Moses) or a wonder-worker (Elijah) of a new and rather special kind. Jesus is no longer to be someone to look back to. And that is why con-fining him in a special experience or a wonderful moment, while religiously and humanly interesting and perhaps stimulating, will not in the end do him justice.

So what kind of presence are we speaking of? The word 'tabernacle' is used in old translations of the Bible at this point, corresponding to *tabernaculum* in Jerome's Vulgate Latin text. Modern translations tend to use 'dwelling', which catches the imagery of the Greek word, *skēnos*, meaning tent. This is the noun that produces the verb, 'pitch one's tent', which John's gospel uses when he describes the Word 'dwelling' among us, literally 'pitching his tent' (John 1:14). This word is supposed to express movement (focus), not solid building (confinement). And yet, from the context, it is clear that Peter wants to have his cake and eat it. He wants to build three dwellings, tabernacles, for the three of them, perhaps so that he can go back there later on, in order to commemorate the event. No wonder none of the evangelists actually names the mountain where it all happened!

The presence of God brings us face to face with how we understand sacraments, where what we are faced with is not people or events, but gestures and actions in a highly symbolic context. In the centenary year of the birth of Dietrich Bonhoeffer (1906–45), it is worth noting his repeated view, discovered through the tragic consequences of protesting against the Nazi regime, that you cannot have God without the world, and you cannot have the world without God.[2] Sacraments are ways of God speaking to us, not through monuments to a remarkable past but as means of grace for the here and now. Water is about washing – and about rebirth. Bread and wine are about eating and drinking. Water is primeval, in that it is there, and requires no special production, whereas bread and wine are the result of our own efforts, in mixing crushed grain with yeast, and crushing grapes so that they can ferment into wine. Thus the Eucharist has from the very start overtones of sacrifice: the elements that are at its heart are the result of 'destroying' the fruits of the field and the vineyard. Oil is another sacramental symbol, used both for healing and for anointing for priestly service, and is likewise the result of crushing olives (or other plants) in order to yield soothing (and sometimes fragrant) oil.

But how is God present? This is quite a theological battleground. But even Thomas Aquinas (1226–74), controversial in his time, and known for working out the (comparatively new) term 'transubstantiation' in relation to the Eucharist, stated categorically that 'He is not in this Sacrament as in a place' and 'the body of Christ is not locally in the Sacrament of the altar.'[3] Ecumenical convergence has moved us away from the caricatures of a Protestant 'real absence' at loggerheads with a Roman Catholic 'Christ on the altar'. As with much else, the broader-sweeping theological approaches of the Christian East have helped towards an understanding of the Eucharist that has movement as well as specificity. The word 'mystery' in the Christian East is not a vague gaze at an icon in a nicely religious frame of mind. It is about having the confidence to believe that God is speaking and acting through baptism, through Eucharist, and through many other ways as well (the East has never confined the number of sacraments to two or seven!). Michael Ramsey (1904–88) provides a succinct answer that draws faith, the cross and the incarnation together: '*Mystery* means that Christ by His body and blood feeds His people with Himself, and that presence of His body and His blood is not the result of the individual's faith, but, like the Incarnation itself, a presence which faith may receive and which unfaith may reject.'[4]

It is, admittedly, one thing for Michael Ramsey to write about the Eucharist in the context of the growing ecumenical consensus of the mid twentieth century, and another thing altogether to stand in the place of Peter in his enthusiasm for what for him and his fellow disciples must have been an unprecedented event. Sacraments, after all, are not necessarily 'special moments' in the feelings of the recipient, and don't have to be in order to function, as Ramsey makes clear: they have to bear repetition, whether once for all for the disciples at the font or week by week at the altar. However, we do have to go back to Peter, and accept that there is part of us that *does* want to stand there with him, and that wants to confine an experience of Jesus within certain boundaries. The trouble is that the harder we try, the more impossible it becomes. Those 'tabernacles', 'dwellings' are unnecessary. They would have been signs of dependence. They would have failed to 'capture' Jesus, because they would have made his 'presence' on a par with the other two figures. Moses and Elijah can come and go. But Jesus goes on for ever, as Matthew makes plain right at the end of his gospel (Matt. 28:20).

The three narratives all say the same thing, but they do it in remarkably different ways. Peter is so overcome by what has happened that he wants to build three dwellings, one for Jesus, one for Moses, and one for Elijah (the same order in all three accounts). But there the resemblances end. Jesus is addressed differently in each of them: Mark calls him Rabbi, Matthew calls him Lord, and Luke calls him Master. Second, the attitude of Peter comes across differently in all three. Mark says that he 'did not know what to say', suggesting that Peter was lost for words; Matthew has the polite insertion, 'if you wish', which mixes well with 'I will make three dwellings' (contrasting with the other two, 'let *us* make'); and Luke has 'not knowing what he said' tacked on at the end, which suggests that Peter spoke without thinking. There is a different kind of relationship indicated by these nuances, which have been picked up by preachers down the ages. And Luke's 'just as they were leaving him' makes Peter's reaction even more circumstantial.

But before we look at these variants in more detail in the context of each overall narrative, we have to ask the question, what about these tents, dwellings, booths? There are three possible points of origin, but none of them entirely fills the bill.[5] The first is the Feast of Tabernacles, which was originally a harvest festival, during which worshippers lived in tents or huts made from leaves and branches, to recall their wandering in the wilderness; but the feast over time developed a more eschatological focus, pointing to God's final redemption (Lev. 23:33–36; Deut. 16:13–15). But, as both Lee and Heil point out, why did Peter not suggest the construction of huts for all six of them, even if he did construe what had just happened to Jesus as a sign of the end? The second option is the Tent of Meeting, where God spoke to Moses outside the Israelites' camp (Exod. 33:7–11; Deut. 31:14–15). On that score, the Transfiguration means that this direct communication between God and the people has been reconstituted and this is why Peter wants three tents built. But, again, it doesn't quite work: why three tents instead of only one? And the third option is to regard these tents as the eternal dwellings for the righteous at the end of all things (cf. *1 Enoch* 39:3–8; *Testament of Abraham* A 20:13–14). But while this matches the heavenly garments of Jesus, Peter has still equated the three of them, placing Jesus on the same level as Moses and Elijah, about whose garments we have heard nothing out of the ordinary. What, therefore, would be the point of such tents?

The only conclusion that can be drawn from these three options is that they provide a basic background but they do not explain what is in Peter's mind, or rather, what the audience is supposed to make of it. For neither the Feast of Tabernacles, nor the Tent of Meeting, nor heavenly dwellings quite fit the context. And this is the conclusion of preachers and commentators down the ages. John Hacket, for example, in his colourful and pastoral way, describes what they might have looked like. He suggests that they were

either booths compacted of arms of trees lopped off from the trunk, called 'attegiae' by the Old Latins, or pleasant arbors of living boughs, which were writhed-in arch-wise over head, and every sprig closed twisted in, to fence off the weather, called 'arbuscula topiaria'; the best shelters to receive these great persons that the poor man could think of, whether the mountain could afford them or no, we have no evidence to make it appear, that was never thought of when he spoke it, for he was so surprised with joy, that he had no leisure to recollect himself, but herein his zeal was very generous, he would fain build another world, and never see this again.[6]

Hacket is commenting on Luke's account, which is more favourable to Peter than Mark, who is apt to be more critical of the disciples. One gets a sense of what these tents, huts, booths, might have looked like. But there is the added doubt expressed about whether the materials for such constructions, however temporary and meagre, would be available on the mountain-top. It all serves to make Peter's enthusiasm all the more impulsive. And, as we shall see shortly with the sermon of Hacket's Anglican seventeenth-century contemporary, Mark Frank, the tents become good examples of how we must understand – and not misunderstand – the life of faith, from the presence of Christ in our institutions and our lives, to the way we celebrate the Eucharist.

But there is more that must be said of these differences in the context of the gospels concerned. Peter's interjection comes as a response (the Greek word means 'reply'), almost as if Jesus has been speaking to the disciples, which is exactly what he wasn't doing. Mark's 'Rabbi' is in stark contrast to Peter's confession of Jesus as the Messiah only some verses earlier (Mark 8:29), and might even indicate that Peter is downgrading Jesus from that unique role into being the same as Moses and Elijah. Matthew, however, depicts Peter calling Jesus Lord when arguing with him after Jesus openly predicted his suffering, death and resurrection (Matt. 16:22). Luke's 'Master', on the other hand, follows a pattern: Peter uses the same term when told (in front of James and John) to cast his nets (Luke 5:4), but after the miraculous catch, he then calls him 'Lord' (Luke 5:8); the disciples call Jesus 'Master' in the storm (Luke 8:24), before he calmed it; and Peter used the same term when Jesus asked who had touched him (Luke 9:33), when the woman with the haemorrhaging was healed. On that score, Peter's 'Master' at this point, the Transfiguration, should be preparing the audience for another revelation.[7]

We are left with three differently nuanced accounts. Mark regards Peter as having made a major misunderstanding of the situation, compounded by the disciples being terrified (the

88

same reaction when Jesus walked on the water, Mark 6:52), whereas Matthew regards it as only of minor significance, because of coming events, and Luke, the most sympathetic of all three, clearly wants us to think that Peter is not really to be taken seriously. All agree on Peter's affirmation that it is 'good', i.e., in the will of God, to be 'here' – a clear echo of the prediction by Jesus immediately preceding the mountain trek (albeit by a few days) that there are some standing 'here' who will see great things (Mark 9:1; Matt. 16:28; Luke 9:27). Matthew's more detached version, with its deference towards Jesus, refers back to Jesus calling him Peter, the Rock, on which the Church will be built (Matt. 16:18), thus putting Peter forward as the one who responds to this vocation by taking the initiative – in this case, a wrong initiative – to build the tents.[8] The Church, however, is not to be built on the mountain of Transfiguration.

Faced with these differences, our task is not to try to discern what originally happened but to take them as essential parts of each gospel narrative. Preachers in the past have sometimes deliberately opted for one version at the expense of another. For example, when we look at the Greek tradition, whereas Basil of Seleucia (d. *c.* 468) emphasises that Peter didn't see the point, John of Damascus (*c.* 675–*c.* 750) can't bring himself to describe him as foolish.[9] But there is one mannerism which has quite a life in sermons both Eastern and Western, and that is for the preacher to address Peter directly at this point. Among the first was Augustine (354–430) in one of his homilies:

> Come down, Peter! You were eager to go on resting on the mountain; come down, 'preach the word, press on in season, out of season, censure, exhort, rebuke in all long-suffering and teaching' [2 Tim. 4:2]. Toil away, sweat it out, suffer some tortures, so that by means of the brightness and beauty of right and good activity, you may come to possess in charity what is to be understood

by the Lord's garments. We heard the praises of charity, you see, when the apostle was being read: 'it does not seek its own advantage' [1 Cor. 13:5]. It does not seek its own advantage, because it gives away what it possesses.[10]

This fashion for addressing Peter was so strong that it is found in the Transfiguration sermon (on the Lucan narrative) by George Whitefield, (1714–70), the evangelical Methodist, where he adopts a characteristically favourable Lucan style: 'Surely, Peter, thou wast not quite awake.'[11] But whichever version is preferred, Peter's motivation is to stay up there and try to hold the moment where it is. And that is to misunderstand the meaning of Transfiguration, whether he didn't know what to say, or didn't know what he was saying, and whether he was trying to be the proper Peter on whom the Church was to be built, or just the spokesman for his colleagues at a point in the proceedings when he thought something should be said and done.

Among the unsung heroes of the seventeenth-century Anglican tradition is Mark Frank (1613–64).[12] Born in a country vicarage, he studied at Pembroke Hall, Cambridge in 1627, where upon graduation he became a Fellow in 1634. His preaching is often compared to that of Lancelot Andrewes, although it is simpler in style. But he was of the Andrewes school of theology, which brought him into trouble with the Roundhead Parliament, and he was ejected from his post in 1643. From this point until the Restoration of the monarchy in 1660, practically nothing is known about his life. But as soon as King and Prayer Book were reinstated in that year, Frank returned to Cambridge. He went on to hold additional posts, including Chaplain to the Archbishop of Canterbury, Canon Treasurer of St Paul's Cathedral, and Archdeacon of St Albans, then part of the London diocese, where he was a colleague of John Hacket (Chapter 3) for a short time. Two years later he was made Master of Pembroke College, and it was during these last two years that the new chapel was built, designed by the architect Christopher Wren (1632–1723), a project in which Frank took a strong personal interest, solid foundations and all.

Among those keen on the Transfiguration was John Cosin (1595–1672), whose writings Frank would have known well.[13] In a series of notes written up in 1660 to prepare for the revision of the Prayer Book, but probably based on earlier work, Cosin drew attention to the feast, describing it as 'ancient', though he notes that the Greek Church kept the feast long before the time of Pope Callixtus III. However, in the 'Durham Book', a text of the Prayer Book printed in 1619 with manuscript notes consisting of corrections, clarifications and additions as he developed them over the years, Cosin proposes something akin to the Danish Lutheran solution: include it in the Epiphany season, and with something like the traditional 6 August lections: 2 Peter 1:15–20 and Matthew 17:1–6. The rationale for Cosin is that the Transfiguration was one of the ways in which Jesus 'manifested' himself.

When we come to Frank's sermon, it is not clear when exactly it was preached.[14] Cosin's Epiphany proposal did not see the light of day, because in any case the August date returned to the Calendar in 1662. Was Frank's sermon preached right at the end of his life (he died, we must remember, in 1664)? Or was it preached earlier in his career, when, perhaps, the feast was kept in a more subdued manner? All we do know is that in the first printed edition of the sermons in 1672, it is referred to as 'a sermon upon the Transfiguration'. Like Hacket (and Whitefield), the Lucan version is used, and Frank's sermon text is Peter's suggestion to build the three tabernacles. From the start, he stresses the importance of prayer, and he likens being on the holy mountain with being present 'at the holy table' (like John Hacket), for it is 'good to be here'; and there is a hint given that this was recent, both at the start of the sermon and later on, which suggests that the sermon might have been delivered at evensong (perhaps on the first Sunday in August?). Frank's sense of the need to savour sacred experiences comes across when he remarks that it is 'good to keep the scent and relish of those heavenly dainties in our souls' – another reference to the Eucharist, that might have taken place that morning.

But for all that Frank places his entire trust in Christ, and sees the Eucharist as central to his life as a Christian, there is much in the sermon that is a sharp warning against the wrong sort of religion, which is hardly surprising in view of the controversies through which he lived. It is indeed good to be with Christ 'in a place of safety', 'when outward blessings glister about us', but more important still that we 'serve the Lord without distraction'. It is good to have our clothing 'white and glistering with him', but Peter still got it wrong. To be 'in the mount only and no more, in honour and high places' is to be near storms and lightning; and the 'mountain of righteousness' is not always a good place to be, not always safe. And he comes to the crunch: 'it is not good always to be here in perpetual and uninterrupted sensible heavenly comforts.' In a passage reminiscent of the first devotional life of Christ (*The Great Exemplar*), written by Jeremy Taylor (1613–67) in 1649, he remarks,

> it is good that Christ, and Moses and Elijah, all should draw sometimes behind the cloud; good sweetness of Law, and prophets, and Gospel too, should be curtained up from us for a while, that we might see our wants, increase our longings, advance our endeavours, and grow more earnest to seek, more careful to pursue after them.[15]

Frank is here articulating the traditional scepticism about special experiences that runs through much Eastern and Western spiritual theology. It trusts in God alone, but is ready to mistrust human instincts, however well grounded. And he takes this further in his discussion of 'tabernacles'. Yes, we should build churches (as Frank did for Pembroke, Cambridge!), and almshouses, and build true religion there, by God's grace. Yes, we should build one for Christ ('make all the provision for Christ to stay with us'), and also one for Moses ('for works as well as faith') and for Elijah ('the prophets must not be shut out of doors'). But there are dangers in the process. One is to seek somewhere higher than Mount Tabor, in order to live there 'as if there were no other world'; to stay there for 'peace and quiet'; 'engrossing Christ only to ourselves' (there is a gospel to live and to share); and to 'make tabernacles, bars and fences, to keep him from doing his office to all the world besides'. Then the wonderful one liner: 'if our retirements hinder us not in our Christian duty, we may retreat into our tents.' And he quotes Jerome on the need to see Gospel, Law and Prophets together. Addressing some of the religious debates of his time, he criticises Roman Catholics for a vision of 'Christ's corporal presence', just as he rounds on extremists who 'dream of the millennary's happiness' which is 'mere talking in our dreams', 'mere castles in the air'. Frank draws attention to sinful passion, indiscretion, natural infirmity, and, above all, excess of zeal. But he ends on a note of deep and lasting joy, with a prayer that we may learn to do and speak what is right for the moment, and 'temper them soberly'. For so will Christ 'tarry with us, and Moses not forsake us, and Elias not depart away out of the mountain from us, till we come to the everlasting hills, to eternal mansions, houses not made with hands, eternal in the heavens'.

Frank's perspective on Transfiguration is both personal and ecclesiological. It is about discipleship and personal faith, with all the pitfalls that religious belief and practice bring. But it is also about living that faith in company with others, which is why he sees the link between Transfiguration and the Eucharist ('the relish of those heavenly dainties'), and the need for the Transfiguration to inform, challenge and even give a constructive critique to our self-understanding as a church. He had suffered for his beliefs by refusing to take the Solemn League and Covenant, which would have torn him away from his monarch (and Church) at a time of civil war. Many others have taken similar choices, or had to take quite different steps in their life of faith. Our own age is, thankfully, a far cry from England in the seventeenth century. And yet there is a cost involved in taking Transfiguration seriously. Our life as individuals and our collective life as a church are placed under the microscope. Building a religious dwelling, liturgical, spiritual, architectural, theological, cannot be an end in itself.

Peter's enthusiasm, however we understand it, remains a vital part of this narrative. It is not a mistake in the story. It is the one incident which is impossible to portray, whether explicitly, or by implication, in an icon, unless we think of those occasions when Peter extends his hand up towards Jesus – as is the case with Theophanes the Greek. The dwellings, tents, shelters, booths simply weren't made. Perhaps Hacket was right to suggest ironically that the materials were not around. Yet it is Peter's sudden enthusiasm which John Armitage Robinson (1858–1933) makes our own in his short five-stanza Transfiguration hymn, written in 1888, with the repeated opening line, "'Tis good, Lord, to be here'.[16] But perhaps in the event the stunning silence which followed is the best answer to Peter's desire to encapsulate this special moment in some kind of basic symbolic form.

I can think of many occasions when I have wanted to do exactly the same. As Christmas Day approached during my illness, the question that kept surfacing was whether I would recover from the infection that had followed one of the courses of chemotherapy. Fortunately, this infection was not as bad as the previous one. But I knew that hospital time is no respecter of time outside – except, of course, in ensuring that doctors, nurses and other staff are scheduled to keep the institution going. Would I get home? In the event, I went home on day release, because it was essential that I return at that stage each night for intravenal antibiotics, i.e., antibiotics that I could not take in the form of pills. So Sarah came and collected me early in the morning, and I went home to the family. We celebrated the Eucharist in the chapel at Bishopsgrove and then sat down to our Christmas dinner. Nothing was said about the fact that I would be returning to my hospital bed that evening. Everyone put their best into the day. We had unforgettable three-part harmony at the Eucharist, and an unforgettable slab of turkey for dinner. Time stood still. September had started in the usual way as if the autumn was just going to be like any other. Then the world had fallen apart with the diagnosis of why I was not feeling quite up to full strength a few days later.

Time stood still, both around the table of the Lord and around the dining table. I can still hear the music we made at the Eucharist, and the laughter we had at the meal. I knew that I couldn't build any tent, or shelter, or hut to commemorate it. But I knew that I could in my mind – and that was all that mattered, as I went back to my bed in the ward, and gave thanks for still being alive. The Eucharist was special, because of the circumstances. But its genius lay in the fact that it held within itself the essential ingredients that make up any other Eucharist anywhere else in the world: gathering, reading from the word, intercession, preparation of the gifts, thanksgiving, communion and conclusion. The simple genius of the rite, with its simple words and actions, spoke volumes about Christ present in our midst, but not located in a mechanistic way. And the relationship between the chapel and the dining room was needed, if only for the one to keep its discreet distance from the other.

Just as the question about Moses and Elijah was 'with whom?', so the question about Peter's enthusiasm is 'what next?' The very fact that those particular shelters were not what was required makes us realise that there is more to play for – the cloud, the voice, and the descent. 'Come down,

Peter', cries Augustine, giving voice to the many people who
have read this narrative and found it both tantalising and
challenging. There *is* a next step – and we have to wait for it.
We need our holy places and our sacred times and seasons,
for this is the framework within which God has both created
and redeemed us. It is a question of focus – and not confining.
John Inge puts much of this into words when he writes of
sacramental encounters:

> The place in which such encounters occur is always
> important to the person who has the experience, and this
> means that the biblical paradigm of people, place, and
> God ... is upheld. In many instances the place can
> become significant to others, too. In such cases the
> encounter is built into the story of the place for the
> Christian community as well as the individual, and this is
> how places become designated as holy. Holy places are
> thus associated with holy people to whom and in whom
> something of the glory of God has been revealed. The
> existence of such holy places should facilitate a sacra-
> mental perception and serve as a reminder that all time
> and place belong to God in Christ – the part is set aside
> on behalf of, rather than instead of, the whole.[17]

Chapter 7

CLOUD

Prayer is the mother of that blessed vision.
(Gregory Palamas, *c.* 1296–1359)[1]

Then a cloud overshadowed them.
(Mark 9:7a)

While he was still speaking, suddenly a bright cloud overshadowed them.
(Matt. 17:5a)

While he was saying this, a cloud overshadowed them, and they were terrified as they entered the cloud.
(Luke 9:34)

Clouds and mountains have a habit of going together. Sometimes the clouds are above or near the top. Sometimes the clouds cover much of the mountain. And at other times the cloud covers only the lower reaches of the mountain, leaving the summit as clear as day. A cloud is a dense mist which is formed out of water in the atmosphere. In its severest form it becomes ice or snow. The more normal forms of cloud are cirrus, the thread cloud, cumulus, the heap cloud, stratus, the flat cloud, and nimbus, the rain cloud. Other classifications are derived from these, the basic shapes of cloud. Their shapes and sizes vary and, of course, the effect of light on clouds can alter their appearance.

It is not clear exactly what form of cloud is being alluded to in the Transfiguration at this point. If we take the view that 'something' happened up there, so far the circumstantial evidence points to a mountain walk among friends, the close companionship (perhaps shared mostly in silence) as the group walked higher, the sudden effect of light on the leader of the group, and the memory of familiar figures illuminating the experience. So far, so good. But from now on, things get a little more strange. We have a cloud, a voice, the disappearance of the cloud, and the walk back down together. It would be pedantic to try to force on the scene an exact description in meteorological terms of the type of cloud that enveloped Jesus. It was obviously not a nimbus, otherwise there might have been some rain. It was probably not a cumulus or heap cloud, as that does not match the narratives either. A thread cloud would not qualify, as it would not have the same effect either. The nearest we can get is a variant of the stratus or flat cloud, called the 'cirrostratus', which is thin and white, and which does not blur the outlines of the sun or the moon, and gives the sky a milky look, though even here, we could only explain the event if there were some distance (some yards) between Jesus and the three disciples. None of the narratives mention distance, although they imply it. Iconography, on the other hand, invariably does – although this is probably in order to encapsulate the whole narrative, rather than defer to some view of the weather conditions that gave rise to this particular part of the overall happening.

Clouds distort reality, especially if one is inside a cloud. What one sees changes in perspective, and sounds echo differently, just as they do when sailing in fog, which is why a foghorn in the pre-radar era became essential in order to determine what was around the ship. The same is true when walking through mists. The atmosphere is different, not just damp or cold. It 'feels' strange. Most people nowadays are more likely to experience it when driving through fog in a car. It's important to see that the lights are on, and that the driver takes care. I have always been at my most terrified (and probably also terrifying!) when I have suddenly unawares had to drive through a patch of fog, because there are occasions when it is impossible to tell how long it is going to last, whether the fog is uniformly thick, or whether there are going to be moments of clarity that come as a blessed relief. The fear that it engenders is not just about whether another car will suddenly loom up and there is a risk of an accident. Fear takes over because of the isolation of being there, in a very different environment, where one has very little control over events.

All that this 'reality check' on the Transfiguration narrative is suggesting is a natural background context to what is essentially a supernatural event – like the other miracles, the transfiguring of the earthly by the heavenly. We can, perhaps, conclude that the four companions probably risked encountering clouds of some sort on their six-hour hike up Mount Hermon, especially if it is supposed to have taken place in spring. A cirrostratus cloud could have swept across the mountain top, whether for a few moments or for longer. Jesus as the leader would probably have reached the summit first, which might explain the distance. Exhaustion can take over, unless another stimulus provides that extra bit of energy that enables the climber to enjoy the achievement of having reached the top, to say nothing of the vistas to the north, south, east and west. We could almost say, if we are trying to relate the narrative to real-life possibilities, that the cloud *intervened*. One could go further and say that the disciples might have been disappointed that it came at all.

Biblical scholars are apt to dismiss the search for what kind of cloud is being referred to at the Transfiguration, but concentrate (as we shall see) on their Old Testament symbolism of the presence of God.[2] Although the Greek word used (*nephelē*) usually means a little cloud, there is a long and worthy tradition in the Old Testament of the cloud as a way of alluding to God's power in creation, as with the rainbow at the end of the Noah narrative (Gen. 9:13) as well as the darkness of the mystery of God as experienced by Moses (Exod. 24:15). It was in a pillar of cloud that God led the people of Israel through the Wilderness by day, and a pillar of fire by night (Exod. 13:21). The cloud motif represents both the distance of God and God's (intermittent) revelation of himself at one and the same time. This is one of the reasons why the Transfiguration is so often seen as embodying both these sides of the paradox: what is called the 'cataphatic' way of speaking of God, which stresses what we *can* say about him, and what is called the 'apophatic' way of speaking of him, which stresses what we cannot say.

Although he did not write a discourse or a homily on the Transfiguration, Maximus the Confessor (*c.* 580–662), a greatly revered theologian of the Greek tradition, used the Transfiguration as a way of illustrating an important distinct truth. There is a *positive* way of interpreting this apophatic (negative) way of speaking of – and knowing – Jesus as the Incarnate Word of God. No words come from the mouth of Jesus at the Transfiguration moment, but he is seen and known, as Andrew Louth has helped us understand.[3] Indeed, when Maximus is reflecting on the three tents, and their aftermath, which could almost be described as an 'apophatic non-event' (my suggestion), he writes as follows:

> These tabernacles represent three stages of salvation, namely that of virtue, that of spiritual knowledge and that of theology. The first requires fortitude and self-restraint in the practices of virtues (by which he means the active life of ascetic struggle): of this the type was Elijah. The second requires right discernment in natural contemplation (by which he means contemplation of the

100

natural order): Moses disclosed this in his own person. The third requires the consummate perfection of wisdom ('theology' means contemplation of God): this was revealed by the Lord.[4]

Maximus is writing specifically of the Transfiguration, which was not yet a festival at Constantinople but was still seen to be an important event in the life of Christ. But there has always lingered in the West a tradition of seeing the Transfiguration more in terms of the life of discipleship and prayer, perhaps because of the lateness of the feast (and its comparative neglect). We have had some examples already, notably in John Hacket and Mark Frank. Yet another example is their contemporary Jeremy Taylor, who takes this more general approach but with imagery indubitably wrested from the Transfiguration: 'Every man that is in this condition of a confirmed grace does not always know it; but sometimes God draws aside the curtains of peace and shows him His throne and visits him with irradiations of his glory, and sends him a little star to stand over his dwelling, and then again covers it with a cloud.'[5]

Here is a broader view, but unmistakably Transfiguration, even Matthean in its tone, complete with the allusion to the star of Bethlehem (Matt. 2:1–12). The net result in experiential terms is both cataphatic and apophatic. We can say things about God incarnate in Jesus Christ but do not and cannot see the whole. And yet even in the reality of not knowing God, when the star is removed behind the cloud, we are still aware of knowing the unknowable. Taylor's 'Great Exemplar' (1649) is a consistently underestimated work, full of penetrating insights into the Christian life. In a strange way, Taylor's 'cloud' reaches back to what is probably one of the greatest works of spiritual theology of the late Middle Ages, the (anonymous) fourteenth century *Cloud of Unknowing*, which was written for contemplatives, and has an overall message similar to Taylor's 'star' and 'cloud', though it delves more deeply into the life of prayer: '[Only if] this secret little love set upon the *cloud of unknowing* be in a ghostly manner the chief of all their work . . . then it is a token that they be called by God to this work; and surely else not.'[6] In their different ways, Maximus, Taylor and the author of *The Cloud* point to the many-layered imagery of this stage in the Transfiguration drama. And we cannot stop trying to imagine what the cloud might have looked like, especially as all the indications from Eastern iconography – Theophanes the Greek in particular – are about a cloud of clarity and light.

But what of the narratives themselves, the inspiration of so much interpretation and speculation? As usual, Mark is brief and to the point, and simply states that the cloud then appeared. But Matthew and Luke give us more – not that the event becomes any less mysterious, because the overall effect is to make it even more so. Matthew has another 'behold' in the Greek, which Luke does not include, although like Matthew he used this demonstrative to point up the appearance of Moses and Elijah as a special event (Luke 9:30). Both Matthew and Luke set the appearance of the cloud while Peter was making the suggestion about the three tents, which has the effect of gently dismissing it. And Luke adds the disciples' fear, as 'they' (all six of them, or just Moses and Elijah?) entered the cloud. Each narrative, then, has a markedly different construction of this episode.

As for the cloud itself, there are two main Old Testament precedents, over and above the fact that it symbolises the presence of God. The Shekinah cloud, according to Evans, 'descends, rises, or remains stationary over the tabernacle, as the localized manifestation of the presence of God', and he cites five passages (Exod. 19:9; 33:9; 34:5; 40:34; 2 Macc. 2:8).[7] Heil takes this interpretation further by listing those occasions when the cloud moves away with people, so that in addition to being an 'epiphanic' cloud, it is also a 'vehicular cloud'. These include Elijah and Enoch going to heaven in a whirlwind (2 Kings 2:11; *1 Enoch* 39:3), as well as occasions in the New Testament, such as the living and the dead caught up in a cloud to meet the Lord (1 Thess. 4:17), the cloud that takes Jesus into heaven at the ascension (Acts 1:9–10), the two prophetic witnesses going up into heaven in a cloud (Rev. 11:12), and the cloud that took Ezra there (Greek *Apocalypse of Ezra* 5:7).[8] It is perhaps easier to see the one kind of cloud moving into the other. In any case, Heil uses this discussion to provide a new interpretation of who exactly is covered by the cloud, and he suggests that it is only Moses and Elijah, since he thinks that the purpose of its appearance is to take them back into heaven at the end. Interesting as this view obviously is, it rests on a partial interpretation of Luke's account when the disciples were afraid as 'they' (Moses and Elijah) entered the cloud.[9]

The more general view is that the cloud, indubitably vehicular (what Heil prefers to call 'oracular'), descended on Jesus, and Moses and Elijah. While the Greek *autous* (them) is ambiguous, Jerome's Latin *intrantibus illis* (as they were entering) can only refer to Moses and Elijah, and not the disciples, the subject of the sentence (*timuerunt*, they feared). Because it is Matthew's narrative that was the most read, not many writers tackle this issue, but two Greek interpreters come to our rescue. These are Timothy of Jerusalem in the sixth century, and Euthymius Zigabenus, the early twelfth-century biblical scholar in his commentary on Luke, where he is quite specific that only Moses and Elijah entered the cloud, because the cloud was heavenly and not earthly, and their entry into it, being supernatural, caused the disciples to be afraid.[10] Modern scholars are less sure, wanting to include the three disciples in the experience.[11] Some would say that it doesn't matter, or perhaps the text might have been clearer. But there is a lot to be said for Euthymius' explanation, based on the overall character of the Transfiguration experience, as perhaps the most convincing. It is perhaps given further support by the direct parallel of language in the Greek version of the Old Testament (the Septuagint) when it refers to Moses entering the cloud at Mount Sinai (Exod. 24:18).

Because Luke's narrative is the fullest, and for some perhaps the most tantalising at this point, it is worth pondering its character. All three evangelists describe the cloud's descent in terms of 'overshadowing' (*episkiazein*), which in the Greek is a pun on the word for tent (*skēnas*); but Luke has already used exactly the same verb in relation to the Holy Spirit 'overshadowing' the Virgin Mary at the Annunciation (Luke 1:35), which places what is happening now in relation to what took place at the start of his gospel, and also expresses the workings of the Holy Spirit, at the Annunciation and in the cloud of Transfiguration. Moreover, like Matthew, as we have observed, Luke's cloud descends while Peter is speaking about the tents, but Luke adds the disciples' fear when Moses and Elijah enter the cloud. Fear in Luke is usually partly awe and partly confusion, such as the shepherds' reaction to the angels at the birth of Christ when the glory of God shone around them (Luke 2:9), when Jesus stills the storm (Luke 8:25), and when the demoniac was healed (Luke 8:35). On each occasion, there was a particular manifestation of the power of God. Here, at the Transfiguration, the disciples' fear is a response to Moses and Elijah being subsumed into the cloud, which we can interpret as (for them) a climactic moment, following the change in Jesus' appearance (Luke's term), and the appearance of the two central figures from Israel's sacred past.

Matthew's narrative is, as we would expect, more soaked in the Moses tradition. This explains his description of the cloud as *phōteinē* (luminous), which matches what he says earlier about the face of Jesus when it 'shone like the sun' (Matt. 17:2). The obvious Old Testament precedent is Moses on Mount Sinai (Exod. 24:15–18; 34:5), making this extra nuance yet one more sign that indicates to the audience that Jesus is the new Moses, with a message and a meaning that both fulfils and extends all that Moses did and taught.

This takes us to Mark's version. Brief and to the point it may be, but his style is once again deceptive. The conclusion one draws from the bald statement that a cloud over-shadowed them is that what we are faced with is a revelation of God. But to what end? How do the disciples take it in? Mark is the evangelist who has a tendency to point up the distance between Jesus and the disciples, in their under-standing of him, and in the way that his identity remains mysterious to the end. It is almost as if Mark's cloud *conceals* Jesus. It descends not only to express the holiness of God but the separateness of Jesus from his followers, both in his identity and in their continuing failure to understand him – hence, as we have pointed out earlier, in the very next chapter James and John themselves ask for special places in the Kingdom (Mark 10:37). As Lee puts it, 'the cloud conceals rather than reveals, covers rather than uncovers.'[12] This lack of comprehension becomes even sharper when we take into account that it is not what the disciples *heard* that is important but what they *saw*, which explains the reference to 'eye-witnesses of his majesty' right at the end of the New Testa-ment (2 Pet. 2:16). That cloud, particularly in Mark, acts as a counterbalance to the dazzling clothing of Jesus earlier: it conceals and covers, rather than reveals and uncovers.

But the cloud not only counterbalances the whiteness and clarity of what has just happened, it renders all the more absurd Peter's spontaneous but embarrassing suggestion that tents should be set up for the three VIPs. And when Luke adds that the disciples were afraid when Moses and Elijah entered the cloud, the implication that can be drawn is that the cloud overshadowed Jesus first, and only then embraced Moses and Elijah. The correlation of that sequence of move-ment is the different ways in which iconography depicts Jesus and the two of them: they are not equal to him, but their presence is vital in order to place Jesus in the context of Israel's unique sacred history, so that *his* uniqueness can be seen for what it is. Maximus' distinction between 'cataphatic' and 'apophatic' springs to mind: we can say things about Jesus, but the fact that we have to acknowledge his 'unknowability' bears testimony to the paradox of Jesus, at one moment wearing dazzling white clothes and the next moment concealed from us. As Lee says:

> Mark confronts the disciples with an identity that is both revealed and concealed at the same time: covered over by their inability to comprehend but even more fundamentally by the very mystery of who and what God is, a God who is made known yet remains elusive (see Mark 4:41). Perhaps there is also a sense of the shadowy cloud protecting the three disciples from a sight too awesome for them to contemplate.[13]

If one is to be really pedantic, one could argue that a luminous cloud cannot overshadow, but it can veil. Perhaps this brings us back to the same paradox, with which each evangelist wrestles in his own way, Mark by his directness, suggesting that the disciples won't get the message in the end, Matthew by his repeated 'beholds' (untranslatable into English) and the reference to luminosity, and Luke by his addition of the disciples being afraid as the two familiar religious figures disappeared from sight. Just as each of the gospel-writers handled Peter's state of mind when he spoke about the tents in a different manner, so here: the cloud comes down, and we are not really sure at all what to make of it. A cloud is a natural phenomenon, because that is what happens on mountains, and there is no way of knowing exactly when some of them appear, how long they will last, when they will part, and when normal patterns of viewing can be restored.

So far, the main historical figures that we have looked at have come either from an era that did not know the feast of the Transfiguration (Jerome, John Chrysostom) or Reformation traditions that had either got rid of the feast or downgraded it, but tried to use the narrative in other ways (Hacket,

Grundtvig, Frank). In some ways, this approach underlines the 'Western' approach of this book. An Easterner would start the other way round, because in the Greek tradition (Orthodox or Catholic), the Transfiguration is one the Twelve Feasts. This prominence owes a great deal to the impetus given by Gregory Palamas[14] (c. 1296–1359), who has left us two major sermons for the occasion. Palamas was probably born in Constantinople, and in 1318 with his two brothers became a monk at Mount Athos. Here he imbibed the spirit of hesychasm, a strong spiritual tradition that went back much earlier to Eastern monasticism in the fourth and fifth centuries, fed by the constant repetition of the 'Jesus Prayer' in tune with the beating of the heart, in order to achieve the union of the mind and the heart. Hesychast monks believed that it was possible to see the divine light, the same light that appeared at the Transfiguration; hence the importance of this event, this feast, to their whole approach to theology. Ordained presbyter in 1326 in Thessalonica, where he had to flee because of the Turkish invasion, he returned to Mount Athos in 1331, and in 1347 was consecrated Archbishop of Thessalonica. He died in 1354 on his way to Constantinople.

As is so often the case, theology develops when confronted by controversy. As a champion of hesychasm, Gregory Palamas defended his position against a Calabrian, Barlaam, who could not understand how human beings could participate in any way in the uncreated divine light of God, in his *Triads in Defence of the Holy Hesychasts*, written c. 1338. One of the main planks in Palamas' defence was the traditional view that we met earlier in Maximus, that just because knowledge of God is apophatic, this does not mean that he is inaccessible to human beings. To put it directly, what would be the point of the disciples being taken by Jesus up the mountain for that experience? Another was the distinction Palamas made between the essence of God, which is beyond human apprehension, and the energies of God, which are the ways in which we can experience and know him. As John Meyendorff puts it, 'the divine energies reflect the unity of the divine essence.'

Both the homilies by Palamas for the feast dwell on the theme of the uncreated light of the Transfiguration, although he does not actually mention hesychasm, nor does he speak of the difference between the essence and the energies of God. He is walking a delicate path, whereas his younger Athonite contemporary, Gregory the Sinaite, allows himself to be more explicit about hesychasm.[15] The fundamental truth for Palamas is that one *can* see the uncreated light with one's own eyes, but they have to be refined by God's grace. This is an entirely different approach from what we have seen in the more 'discipleship' orientation of Hacket, Frank and Grundtvig, and also in Jerome and Chrysostom. It serves as a kind of wedge between reading the Transfiguration as a gospel narrative, and turning it into a major feast, and then investing it with such a specific spiritual load.

Palamas begins Homily 34 by attacking 'heresiarchs' who, he says, try to delve too deeply into the details of texts without pondering their deeper meaning. From that approach we must flee, in order to celebrate the Transfiguration. It is clear that the gospel text begins with the promise to those standing around (Matt. 16:28), which provides him with the opportunity of identifying them as the three chosen to go up the mountain. There is no difference between Matthew and Mark's 'six days' and Luke's 'eight'. These correspond to

> our senses that work in a sixfold manner, for we have five senses but added to these in accordance with the senses, is the uttered word which activates that sixfold energy of our senses. But the Kingdom promised to the saints is not only above sense, it is even beyond speech, and for this reason – for after these sixfold senses have come to a happy end, and in that ending the worthy are enriched in the seventh [state], then is the Kingdom of God revealed in the eighth [state] in a power of even greater energy,

which is the power of the Spirit of God, through whom the saints are found worthy of beholding the Kingdom of God.

Then he encapsulates his entire theology of Transfiguration: 'He gave to those who can see, the power to look on invisible things, having previously cleansed them of deadly and soul-destroying defilement, which is sin.' And this is why those who teach that 'the chief apostles saw the light of the Lord's transfiguration by a sensory and created power' are misguided. All is gift from God – and nothing else. But how do we get there?

Throughout, Palamas stresses the place of prayer; hence his belief that 'prayer is the mother of that blessed vision', and the importance of Luke's insistence on prayer as the reason for the journey (Luke 9:28; cf. 29). It was prayer that brought them there, just as it was prayer that lay at the heart of Jesus' teaching and miracles. But 'Christ was transfigured not by receiving something he did not have before, nor by being changed into something he previously was not, but as manifesting to his disciples what he really was, opening their eyes and from blind men making them see again.' We are back to selection, and the mountain-trek not being for all, either then or now. It is presented as a challenge, not an easy invitation. Jesus' appearance changed in prayer, and it was the light of the Godhead that was revealed. And he ends with a call to the worshippers to 'make our way towards the illumination of that light', with our garments cleansed, so that we may approach the Trinity itself.

Palamas' other Transfiguration homily is more general in approach, adhering less to the narrative. It opens with a string of biblical quotations about the light of the sun, but with the same theme of spiritual ascent. The light of God is not inaccessible, for the cloud on the mountain was clear. For Palamas, the heart of Transfiguration is the combination of light and cloud, the same paradox that we see in the

evangelists' differing treatments of the overshadowing cloud.
And he dares to speak of the essence of God, which we are
unable to gaze upon. The disciples *were* able to gaze on 'that
light' but only partially. He ends with a summary of the
purpose of the Transfiguration, which is about us as much as
it is about Jesus, because of his inclusion of the three chosen
disciples in the experience:

> We believe, as we were taught, that the saints beheld and
> had fellowship not with the essence of God but rather
> with his kingdom and glory, his radiance, his mystical
> light and his divine grace. We press on towards the
> radiance of that light of grace so that we might know and
> venerate the threefold light of the deity that ever shines
> as one; a mystical ray of one nature in three hypostases
> (persons). And we lift up the eyes of our mind towards
> the Word who now sits with his body above the vaults of
> heaven, sitting in glory at the right hand of the majesty.

Light is the hermeneutical key for Palamas on the Transfiguration. And it is this theme that pervades his teaching, both
in these two sermons, and in the 'Triads' written to defend
hesychasm from rationalistic attack. What we are encountering here is a subtle development of monastic spirituality, a
greater weight given to what was once a simple word, *hēsuchia*, silence, tranquillity, which was defined a few centuries
earlier by John of Damascus (*c.* 675–*c.* 750) in his sermon for
the feast as 'the mother of prayer'.[16] The question Palamas
asks – and answers, on his own terms – is the way in which
that uncreated light can be apprehended by humans. It is not
through sensory means; in that respect he complements
Euthymius' view, noted earlier of Luke's account, that the
disciples remained outside the cloud because the whole event
was of a supernatural order. And although, unlike Andrew of
Crete (*c.* 660–740), he does explicitly mention *theōsis* (divin-
isation), the term increasingly used of redemption in Greek
theology (cf. 2 Pet. 1:9, sharing the divine nature), the theme

runs between the lines of both homilies; at the end of the second, he refers to the light as 'God-making'.[17] McGuckin helps us to see far more than Palamas implicitly defending his hesychast monks in these two homilies: a whole pattern of epiphany, of spiritual growth in holiness and the moral life, of cross and resurrection, falls from these pages.[18]

There have been many occasions in my life when I have tried to picture in my mind what the Transfiguration really looked like. What are the evangelists trying to say? What are those icons trying to depict? What is it that we are really trying to do, whether we are reading the narrative in connection with Lent or celebrating an August festival? Again and again I am taken not to the disciples, nor Moses and Elijah, nor even Jesus' face and dazzling clothes, nor yet to the episodes we have yet to look at, namely the voice and the descent. It is the *cloud* that I keep returning to. One of the reasons, I suspect, is precisely because clouds intimate both the height and distance of God and at the same time the mysterious way in which he reaches down to us – hence the continued association of the cloud with the Holy Spirit. Clouds come and go, they part because they cannot stay the same – and there are occasions when I have vivid proof of this fact of life when I sometimes look outside the windows of an aeroplane.

The cloud is a way of envisaging God's *movement*. Much of my life of faith is lived in varying strands of well-intentioned confusion. And that was brought home to me all through my illness with leukaemia. I never questioned God, but I questioned the details and the implications of what believing in him meant for me, for my family, for my friends. I lay there in that bed, whether in shock, or loneliness, or pain, or worry, or in nothingness, and the cloud image of my God meant more than anything else. The cloud was 'there', and there were times when it was clear and light, and there were times when it was distant and meaningless. But it was – and is – a cloud unlike any other. I could press the image further and say that there were times when God rained on me, when he thundered at me, when the lightning flashed. But he was still God. And I was still 'there' as well. Silence, my solitude, even in the moments of restlessness, mental as well as physical, became the transforming mother of my prayer.

The question posed by the three tents, the three tabernacles, was 'what next?', because they lead on to the next stage through the sheer fact of not quite being 'the order of the day'. By contrast, the question raised by that luminous cloud, through which the light shines, is 'what?' What is God, in terms of my discipleship, albeit in company with other people, whether I can get on with them or not? And that brings the cloud right down into all our confusions and muddles. Evelyn Underhill (1875–1941) moved from agnostic to convinced Christian in the earlier part of the last century, pioneering the way for a more integrated ministry for women in the Church. She helped to make the life of prayer something real and (in the best sense) 'accessible', and she was always ready to debunk shallow alternatives to the real thing. In a series of retreat addresses delivered in 1932, she has this to say about *God* taking the initiative, at *his* pace, and in *his* way:

> The mystics keep telling us that the goal of prayer and the goal of our hidden life which should itself become more and more of a prayer, is union with God. We use that phrase often, much too often, to preserve the wholesome sense of its awe-fulness. For what does union with God mean? It is not a nice feeling we get in devout moments. That may or may not be a by-product of union – probably not. It can never be its substance. Union with God means every bit of our human nature transfigured in Christ, woven up into its creative life and activity, absorbed into his redeeming purpose, heart, soul, mind and strength. Each time it happens it means that one of God's creatures has achieved its destiny.[19]

Chapter 8

VOICE

This is my Son, not adopted but my own, not temporal but eternal, not inferior but equal, not from elsewhere but from the same substance.

(Peter the Venerable, 1092/94–1156)[1]

And from the cloud there came a voice, 'This is my Son, the Beloved, listen to him!' Suddenly when they looked around, they saw no one with them any more, but only Jesus.

(Mark 9:7b–8)

And from the cloud a voice said, 'This is my Son, the Beloved, with him I am well pleased; listen to him!' When the disciples heard this they fell to the ground and were overcome by fear. But Jesus came and touched them, saying, 'Get up and do not be afraid.' And when they looked up, they saw no one except Jesus himself alone.

(Matt. 17:5b–8)

Then from the cloud came a voice that said, 'This is my Son, my Chosen, listen to him!' When the voice had spoken, Jesus was found alone.

(Luke 9:36a)

113

When I came out of hospital for the first time after a month away from home, I was looking forward to seeing familiar things again after the most difficult time I'd had in my life. Foremost in my mind was how our border terrier would react to my arrival. Unfortunately, the Bible doesn't like dogs at all. One could almost say that it is fundamentally 'doggist' in character, because whenever those animals are mentioned, it seems to be in a context (or as a term) of abuse. Noah does not have the advantage of their comfort or use, and quite early on they are regarded as beasts that tear other animals apart (Exod. 22:31). It is just possible that the dogs who licked Lazarus' sores outside the rich man's house (Luke 16:21) were domesticated house dogs, but more likely to be dirty street dogs. The New Testament even ends on a doggist note, the heavenly city having nothing to do with them (Rev. 22:15). But I set that cultural conditioning aside as I went through the front door, wondering what sort of welcome I would receive. I had been warned that the fact that I smelt of hospital would probably affect him, as surely it did. But before I had got very far, great excitement barked at me – because he had heard my voice, in every sense 'his master's voice'.

Voices are essential aspects of our identity. I was once told that in the Coptic monasteries in the Egyptian desert, the abbot often decides who will read the lessons at the daily offices, and will listen carefully to the tone and timbre of the voice of the monk in question, because he is able to tell from how he is reading how he is feeling, what the state of his spiritual life is at the time, and even whether he is unwell. In a community where folk are well known to each other, perhaps this goes without saying. When I meet colleagues or speak with them on the phone, I can usually tell if something is troubling them, and on some occasions I might even find out what the reason is! The voice is a giveaway sometimes, and the harder we try to conceal our true feelings in speaking, the more likely it can be that we betray those innermost feelings in how we say what we are supposed to be saying. My own dog can tell if I am upset, not just from my voice, but from what he senses, as animals have highly developed instincts that make humans almost amateurs in the game of second-guessing what is going on around us.

But when we come to the voice at the Transfiguration scene, we leave behind these areas of familiar living. All that the New Testament narratives say is that a voice came from the cloud. No identity is provided – even though what the voice tells us is the identity of the personality at the centre of the drama – he is God's Son – and what the disciples are to do about it – listen to him. No one actually says whose the voice is, and there is as much background information about the identity of the origin of the voice as there was earlier about the identity of the two visitors from Israel's past. In other words, we are left to assume that this is the voice of God, for it can be no other.

Yet more mysterious is how the voice is depicted in icon-ography. In an earlier chapter, we observed that the sugges-tion by Peter to build three tents, one for Jesus, one for Moses and one for Elijah, was one episode which it was impossible to depict, even by implication – unless, that is, we try to read it into the hand gesture of Peter at the foot of the mountain towards Jesus at the top. But with the voice, we are in a dif-ferent sort of dilemma. A voice cannot be painted. But the context of what it is saying certainly can be painted. In the icon by Theophanes the Greek, the voice of God is all around, as in the other Transfiguration icons. In the case of Theo-phanes, the voice seems to 'speak' from the circular mandorla behind the figure of Jesus, as if it were bringing the Christ-figure before the human race that is represented by his three chosen followers, in order to show this new identity, and the obedience to his teaching that those followers are now enjoined to carry out. Andreas Andreopoulos rightly distin-guishes between the circular and the oval mandorlas, sug-gesting that the circular shape points to an inclusive glory, whereas the oval shape points to a more exclusive glory.[2]

Theophanes combines the circular shape with the flashings of light, perhaps a way of depicting both the voice and the luminous cloud that hovers momentarily on the mountain. This is the nearest we get to a voice being 'painted'.

But the voice speaks nonetheless. Perhaps in 'painting' it, the artist has hit upon something that helps the Westerner who is not brought up on icons in quite the same way as Easterners to discern something of the way the 'voice of God' functions in our lives. When my dog heard my voice for the first time for just over four weeks, weeks that were not without anxiety for him as he had missed me and had picked up the anxiety in the house from other members of the family, he recognised immediately who it was because it was familiar. But the voice of God? How familiar is that?

The disciples are neither described in the narratives nor depicted in the icons as understanding immediately exactly what is going on, as if the voice of God were familiar, recognisable, part of the religious culture. What is happening here is something quite different and new, however much the mountain experience has a point of reference in the Old Testament, whether with Moses (Exod. 12:18) or Elijah (1 Kings 19:12). No description is given of the kind of voice that they heard. What is more important than its tone and style is what it actually says: 'This is the one, not Moses, and not Elijah, you must listen to, because he is my Son.' By implication, therefore, and not by candid announcement, the identity of the voice is made clear. It is neither Moses speaking directly with God on the mountain-top, nor Elijah hearing that voice neither in the wind, nor the fire, nor the earthquake, but in the 'sound of sheer silence'. In each of those cases, there is an elusive quality to the way God operates with the two characters in question. Here, there is another kind of elusiveness, an elusiveness that is about Jesus' identity and mission. He is 'my Son' (but what, exactly, is the cash value of that?) and the disciples are to listen to him (but what, exactly, is the purport of his teaching?).

116

The voice, therefore, points to Jesus, while at the same time engaging the disciples in the unfolding drama of Jesus' life, a drama that seems to continue to elude them. It is not a voice from of old, a voice in the memory that can be conjured up and quickly identified ('Oh, that must be God's voice, why didn't I think of it sooner?'). It is a voice of implication, not explication, a voice that speaks succinctly, and without going into lengthy details. It is a voice that points the audience, the worshipper, back to Jesus, whom 'alone' the disciples are soon to see.

But all this raises the question, how do we 'hear' the voice of God in our lives? I tend to work with voices in terms of comparison, so that if I listen to a new actor on television, I think in terms of whose voice that person's is like. Comparison is an essential part of living. It helps us extend the boundaries of our experiences at the same time as deepening them. And if I want to think of what the voice of God is like, then I start thinking more of the kinds of things he has said to me before, and so a small repertoire begins to build up: help here, caution there, encouragement over yonder, and reproof back there. In fact, if I really want to encapsulate the voice of God, I am brought back again to the second part of the Lord's Prayer, when I pray for sustenance for today, forgiveness for yesterday, and protection in the future.[3] I don't go easily for special 'voices', since I know what it is to mistrust my instincts, and I know what it is to see my knowledge as partial (1 Cor. 13:8). I may 'hear' a voice speaking inside me on certain occasions, and I am thankful for them. But I would not presume to expect that voice to speak on every occasion. Hence my basic point of reference, from the teaching of Jesus (Matt. 6:9–13), that God 'speaks' through our hallowing of his name, our praying for the coming of his Kingdom, and the doing of his will, all of these 'on earth as in heaven', for that is what God is like. And from those three close-knit petitions to 'Our' (and not just 'my') Father, I go on to pray for daily bread, forgiveness, and the blessing of his guiding hand in the future. For that reason, the Jesus whom I see in that gold-white mandorla is the same Jesus who keeps teaching me to *pray*. For that is the best way I can 'listen' and 'attend' to him. My many words and my teeming mind have to be – gently but firmly – subjugated to a higher and a simpler and a deeper way of being.

The three disciples now hear a voice 'from the cloud' which tells them who Jesus is and tells them to listen to him. This is what Heil calls the 'pivotal mandate' which is intended to turn their minds back to what they have seen and experienced of Jesus already, and to look forward to what is to come.[4] They no longer see Moses and Elijah, but only Jesus. It's 'this one' that they must heed, and no one else. But the variants are of more than passing interest. Mark, as usual, goes straight on with his narrative ('then'), but Matthew and Luke set this episode closely following the previous – Peter was 'still speaking'. The voice, apparently, came swiftly on Peter's crass suggestion about the tents. Then there are differences in what the voice says, and here there is an important point of comparison with the three baptism narratives (Mark 1:11; Matt. 3:17; Luke 3:22). In all three, the voice comes 'from the cloud', symbol of God's presence, whereas at the baptism of Jesus it came 'from heaven', God's dwelling place. With Mark, the voice at the baptism said 'You are my Son, the Beloved; with you I am well pleased'; here the voice says, 'This is my beloved Son; listen to him!' With Matthew, the voice at baptism said, 'This is my Son, the beloved, with whom I am well pleased'; here the voice says, 'This is my Son, the Beloved; with him I am well pleased; listen to him!' And with Luke, the voice at baptism said, 'You are my Son, the Beloved; with you I am well pleased'; here the voice says, 'This is my Son, my Chosen; listen to him!'

Mark and Luke agree that whereas at the baptism, the voice from heaven addresses Jesus, here on the mountain it addresses the onlookers. Mark's two versions resemble each other, the difference being that Jesus is 'well pleasing' at his baptism, but not at the Transfiguration. Luke makes Jesus 'chosen' (*eklelegmenos*, a perfect passive participle) here, whereas he is 'beloved' at the baptism. Matthew's versions are the two that resemble each other most closely, for he is beloved and well-pleasing in both, and the voice from heaven does not address Jesus, but the onlooker – as at the Transfiguration. Picking over these variants is a fruitful exercise, particularly in view of each gospel writer's style and approach. In all three cases, the voice from the cloud corrects Peter's misinterpretation of what is really happening, but each of them provides a slightly different nuance to Jesus' identity. All imply that Jesus is the Son of God, but in different ways. The title, after all, is not necessarily messianic. With Mark, however, it is heightened by being placed right at the start of the gospel (Mark 1:1), and it appears thereafter at specific places: the demoniac knows exactly who Jesus is before he is healed (Mark 5:7); Jesus admits to the high priest who he is (Mark 14:6); and it is the (Gentile) centurion who comments on his death with a confession of his identity (Mark 15:39). All these are key moments in Jesus' life, and the Transfiguration statement here needs to be seen in that light.[5]

With Matthew, the close similarity with the baptism must be deliberate, explaining the comment made by Bede (*c.* 673–735) that the Transfiguration at this point 'clarifies' the Trinity, similarly revealed at the baptism, with the Holy Spirit in the cloud and the Father in the voice.[6] This is heightened by Matthew's addition of the response of the disciples: they fall down with fear, a posture frequently taken up in iconography. Jesus' response, after all, is in keeping with the rest of Matthew's gospel. He approaches them, moves towards them, a verb used frequently by him when people are approaching Jesus in a suppliant manner (e.g. Matt. 5:1; 8:2). This time, however, the roles are reversed.[7] Jesus is making the formal approach, the other occasion when he does this being when he approaches the disciples on another mountain – in Galilee after the resurrection (Matt. 28:18). Then he touches them, in the same way that he does for the purpose of healing others (e.g. Matt. 8:3), but this is the only occasion when the verb is used *not* in relation to healing. And third, he tells them to rise and not be afraid – the verb for 'rise' being the same one used of his own resurrection (Matt. 16:21; cf. 26:46).

Matthew is more explicit than the other two gospels about the psychological effect of the event on the three disciples. One can almost imagine them rubbing their eyes before looking 'up' and, as Matthew emphasises, seeing Jesus 'himself alone'. Matthew's use of the word 'behold' no fewer than three times around this point only serves to heighten the drama. All this needs to be seen in the context of Peter's confession of Jesus at Caesarea Philippi (Matt. 16:16), when Jesus responded by saying that he would found his Church on Peter. For Matthew, Jesus is 'well pleasing' as the fulfilment of Israel's past; before the baptism, he has been heralded by the coming of the magi, and with the light of a star guiding them to the newborn saviour (Matt. 2:1–12). And as we look forward to the events of the cross, Matthew's dramatic addition of the earthquake (and not just his death) causes the soldiers to comment that he was 'God's Son' (Matt. 27:51–53). Jesus is the new Moses (cf. Septuagint Deut. 18:15), who was promised of old.

Luke's account is the gentlest of all, in tune with his more favourable gloss on Peter's suggestion about the tents – he didn't know what he was saying (Luke 9:33b). No high drama with the disciples – Jesus 'was found alone' when the voice had spoken. But in Luke's gospel, who are the people who 'knew' Jesus' identity? So far not many: Mary, his mother (Luke 1:32, 35), Jesus himself, at his baptism (Luke 3:22), the devil, when Jesus was in the wilderness (Luke 4:3, 9), and the demons who were cast out by Jesus (Luke 4:41; 8:28). Jesus is thus proclaimed as far more than Moses and Elijah, and the disciples have to realise that 'Master' (Luke 9:33), the description used by Peter earlier when speaking about the

120

tents, will not do. That Jesus is 'well-pleasing' means that he is in the same line as God's 'servant' of old. That word 'chosen' refers back to the baptism, even though it is not used there: he was identified then, and he is re-identified now: the same Greek word is used in the Septuagint in the First Servant Song (Isa. 42:1).

All three narratives direct the disciples to 'listen' – a word that reverberates in different ways in each of the gospels. Mark uses the term more frequently. Jesus commands the people to 'listen' (Mark 4:2–3), and it is used several times thereafter in the same context (Mark 4:9, 23, 24; 7:14; 8:18). With Matthew, Jesus is the successor to Moses, but the disciples are to listen to him in a different way, because of who he is; like Mark, 'listen' recurs throughout his gospel (Matt. 7:24, 26; 10:14, 27; 11:15; 13:9, 13, 14, 16, 43). Luke uses the word 'listen' with equal insistence (Luke 8:8, 18; 10:39; 11:28; 14:35). Although, in Luke, the disciples have not heard the details of the conversation that took place between Jesus and Moses and Elijah, they are from now on to attend to him. With all three, the audience, the worshippers, are being exhorted to look at the whole Christ, which means seeing clues for the inner meaning of that identity in what he has said already, by way of prediction of his suffering and death, and in what is yet to come.

What is most curious of all in these narratives is Jesus' silence. Even Matthew's addition of the scene where he approaches the disciples, touches them, commands them to rise and not be afraid, is about calming them down in the aftermath of what has happened. If there is any hint in what he does about his identity, it is perhaps to indicate lack of surprise on his part, and a way of showing that it is the *disciples* who themselves need to hear the good news and to digest it. And this is the point of the scene: Jesus' silence, and the disciples' – the Church's – need to hear the gospel in all its fullness, not as good teaching ('Rabbi', 'Lord', 'Master'), but as words from God himself, spoken through his Son, in the

121

power of the Spirit. Luke does not use the term 'Son of God' very often, which underscores its appearance here. The title occurs more frequently in Mark and Matthew. But the Transfiguration brings out its full meaning. Jesus is God's Son, but this is not a sudden heavenly award. He is going on to suffer and to die – and that is what has to be (Luke 24:7, 26). Transfiguration and cross belong together. Moses died a natural death, and Elijah was taken up into heaven. Jesus is different. As Eduard Schweizer remarks, 'Any visions which could point to the dawning of the end are meant only to indicate the dimension in which one should view those things which will happen to Jesus in his Passion.'[8]

Bede's view that the Transfiguration 'clarifies' the portrayal of the Trinity given at the baptism is too important not to be taken up by later writers. These include Rabanus Maurus (c. 780–856), Ralph of Laon (twelfth century), and Peter of Celle (d. 1156). This interpretation also appears in the East, in Andrew of Crete (c. 660–740), although other Eastern preachers see in this part of the drama the outworking of the Son's 'being of the same substance' with the Father, as we read in Timothy of Jerusalem (sixth century).[9] The cloud needs the voice to interpret its true meaning, the voice of the Father declaring the Son's uniqueness, bound to him, in the power of the Holy Spirit. Without the voice, the cloud remains a cloud, without the final context which is attested by the voice. It is not hard to see why subsequent doctrinal formulations were read into this 'pivotal' moment in the gospels.

The one man whose name is most associated with the Transfiguration in the medieval West is Peter the Venerable, who was born in 1092/94, educated by the Benedictines of Sauxillanges, part of the Cluny 'Congregation' (group) of the Order, and became a monk in 1109. He was elected Abbot of Cluny in 1122 and remained so until his death in 1156.[10] His contribution to the 'Cluniacs' and the wider Catholic Church was immense. He standardised their constitutions, translated the Qur'an into Latin, and made several journeys, to Spain, Italy and England. At that time, the Transfiguration feast was only kept sporadically in the West, and it is clear from his writings that he was a great enthusiast for its wider adoption. In his time, there was a Cluniac community on Mount Tabor, founded by the Crusaders.

In 1132, Peter decreed that the feast should be observed throughout the entire Cluniac Congregation, and it appears that he wrote the antiphons and responsories for the offices. Some of the hymns (on the theme of light) date back further, but his sermon was so influential that parts of it were included in the Office itself. Richard Pfaff, in his study of new feasts in late medieval England, has shown that the Transfiguration was celebrated by some Cluniacs before Peter's time (on the one hand), and provides evidence to suggest that not everyone immediately obeyed Peter's directive that it should be celebrated (on the other). As Jean Leclercq notes, Peter's office is characterised by great simplicity, and its inspiration is entirely biblical. This is in line with his preaching, which avoids the allegorical style of many of his contemporaries. But he manages to intertwine biblically inspired verses with theological commentary: for example, in the night office, whose responsories dwell on the voice on the mountain, suddenly we are taken into the world of Bede some centuries earlier, where the Trinity is discerned both in the baptism of Jesus in the Jordan and at the Transfiguration.[11] Peter's sermon shows every sign of being a set-piece production. One can well imagine it having been preached, but the form in which it has come down to us shows signs of wider use, beyond the liturgical occasion in question. The studious abbot, anxious to promote the life of study so that it would become a hallmark of his communities, fills the pages of this sermon with his love and devotion for the feast.

The sermon begins on the Johannine theme of the light of the glory of the incarnate Christ (John 1:14), which takes him straight to Christ's baptism, 'this is my Son, my Beloved' (Matt. 3:17). And if he has a text for the whole sermon, it is this christological affirmation. He then draws in the three accounts of the Transfiguration. The three disciples represent the Trinity (following Jerome centuries before), but he later adapts one of the other Jerome interpretations, based on their names: Peter recognised Jesus, James was the supplanter, and John was full of the grace of God.[12] He then works out these three associations, using the rhetorical device of repetition, and reaches the end of this part of his discussion by referring to the two 'sons of thunder', and to Peter as the chief pastor of the Church. The gospel narrative is followed as he comments on Jesus taking them up the mountain, with references to Jesus' teaching and healing ministry. Using (mainly) Matthew's account, Peter concentrates on the light of the Transfiguration, as a sign of Christ's body being 'deified'. This is a significant word to find in the Latin West, which reveals the extent of Eastern influence on Peter's apprehension of what Transfiguration means, for he uses the same word on two later occasions in the sermon, both of them in relation to Jesus. But the implication is clear: Jesus' body is 'deified', and that is our calling as well.

Following in the footsteps of earlier preachers, he addresses Peter the apostle direct, but in Lucan rather than Marcan tones. Why are you doing this? Why do you want to stay up here? And in the catalogue of future possibilities he mentions death and passion, the redemption of the world, resurrection and ascension into heaven. It can't be good to be here if that is what all this is going to lead to. The sermon is clear in its handling of the gospel narratives: Transfiguration has to lead to suffering and death, and resurrection and glory. The result of all this is that the three tabernacles take on a new meaning: they represent the Trinity.

We now come to the cloud and the voice, which clearly inspires Peter further. No sooner has he quoted the verse in question than he calls upon patriarchs, prophets, apostles, the departed, the heavenly ones – all of them – to come and be present. For Moses came from below, and Elijah from above, a motif we encountered in the homily by John Chrysostom.[13] All are called to come and recognise Christ as the Son of God, the one who is to suffer and to die, to rise again and ascend into heaven. And at this point, the repetition of 'this is my son' (*'hic est filius meus'*) becomes the dominant note until the end of the sermon. 'I made this flesh, I did not beget it', says the voice, summarising many rivers of theological ink in four Latin words, *'hanc [carnem] feci, non genui'*. He combines the identity of the Son with the reality of the Trinity: 'No difference or variation is felt in our Trinity.' The word 'beloved' (*dilectus*) is given the full treatment, because Peter wants to show that this is a different form of love from human love. This is the love that conquers sin, human beings at their worst; and he cites God coming to the point where he regrets having created humanity (Gen. 6:6). 'This is my Son, not adopted but my own, not temporal but eternal, not inferior but equal, not from elsewhere but from the same substance.'

This leads Peter to his conclusion, which is an act of thanksgiving to the Trinity: 'We thank you, highest Trinity, we thank you, true unity, we thank you, only goodness, we thank you, benign deity.' From praising God, it moves on to giving thanks for our salvation, in that we did not perish, but have been given everlasting life. Prayer to all three members of the Trinity at once was not a feature of patristic liturgy, but it was not unusual in Peter's time. From the ninth century onwards, prayers to the Trinity began to appear at the offertory which the priest recited silently while placing the bread and wine on the altar.[14] Such a background may also have suggested to Peter the need to make some kind of reference to the Eucharist – a 'holocaust of jubilation'. He invokes each member of the Trinity; all three co-operate in our salvation. And the sermon ends with a series of fresh repetitions of *hodie* – 'today', heed Christ's teaching, be saved, and enter the inheritance prepared for us (Matt. 25:41).

For Peter the Venerable, the Transfiguration is indeed a kind of summary of the whole gospel. It is not for nothing that this sermon is the first in the collection attributed to him, which is a sign of the importance given to it by him, or at any rate by those who put them together for circulation, either during his lifetime or after his death. There can be little doubt that we are breathing at least some of the air of the Eastern tradition, where 6 August had been kept as a feast since the seventh century in Constantinople, and even earlier in the Holy Land. So strong is he on light and the identity of Jesus as uttered by the voice that he does not have time to deal with the remaining verses of the narrative. This sermon comes from a time when words were valued and trusted rather more than they are in today's West. But Peter does not leave us up there in glory. His ending has a moral force – we are challenged to live Christ-like lives as a consequence of taking part in that vision.

The voice has spoken, and the disciples then only see Jesus. The familiar figures from the past, the religious tradition, and all that is routine, that gets in the way of the uniqueness of Jesus, disappears. It has come and gone, which makes even more of an impact than if Moses and Elijah had *not* appeared at all. If we follow Matthew's account, the disciples respond with fear, whereupon Jesus comes to them, touches them, and tells them to rise and not be afraid. If we follow Mark and Luke, Jesus says and does nothing. To 'see Jesus alone' can be a hard thing, because it means excluding all that is secondary, all that is less than him, all that gets in the way. For many of us, such a purging experience may be a once-in-a-lifetime event, whether it is a bereavement, a serious illness, or a calling that can only require the answer 'yes'. Those kinds of challenges can be dramatic and usually are, although when one looks back on them, they tend with time to fade into the distance, and be absorbed into the memory as part of oneself, one more part of one's own pilgrimage of faith.

When we looked at the 'Cloud', the question posed was 'what?' What is the meaning of this cloud, and what is it trying to do and say? The 'Voice', however, raises a different kind of question – 'who?' Whom are we speaking about? The answer is Jesus, but how we get there is by no means straightforward. Faith for the vast majority of people is often quite a struggle. The answers are not always obvious or apparent. Of course there are times when we ask 'O let me hear thee speaking/ in accents clear and still' (to quote the third stanza of the hymn, 'O Jesus, I have promised/ to serve thee to the end'),[15] and the voice somehow speaks. But there are also times when I don't know what the will of God is until I have done it. There is seldom a blinding moment. For me, Transfiguration occasionally does take place upon the mountain, my recent illness being an obvious exception. Transfiguration may take me up different kinds of mountains, the scaling of which may well be spiritually (if not also physically) exhausting. But most of the time, it is about daily living, when the voice of God speaks in rather more mundane ways.

For much of my time in hospital, and for much of my time in my daily work, Transfiguration is about silence, about waiting for God to speak. For that purpose, my chapel is invariably a context in which I can share my silence with God's silence. In a world of overpopulated minds, news bulletins by the second, and an information technology explosion, the absence of all those distractions is a refreshing change. Much of the time, however, it can become quite hard work to purge those distractions away. This is not done by sitting on them, but by recognising them for what they are. Occasionally, God will go so far as to *use* them as a way of telling me something I have missed, like a fresh approach to an old problem. But the silence is what I value most. It is rather like some of the visits to my sickbed by close family when I was seriously ill at the start of treatment. They simply came and sat, and were content not to feel compelled to *say* something all the time, a particularly clerical temptation.

In a recent book about communication between people, Peter Shaw tells the story of Mother Teresa being interviewed by a journalist about her life and faith. She was asked what she said to God when she prayed. 'I don't say anything,' she replied. 'I just listen.' 'And when you listen,' said the interviewer, 'what does God say?' 'He doesn't say anything,' she replied. 'He just listens.' Before the bewildered journalist could say anything more, she added, 'And if you don't understand that, I can't explain it to you.'[16]

Chapter 9

DESCENT

*When we looked at him he did not appear the same way to all
who saw him, but rather according to their individual capacity
to receive him.*

(Origen, c. 185–c. 254)[1]

*As they were coming down the mountain, he ordered them to tell
no one about what they had seen, until after the Son of Man
had risen from the dead.*

(Mark 8:9)

*As they were coming down the mountain, Jesus ordered them,
'Tell no one about the vision until after the Son of Man has been
raised from the dead.'*

(Matt. 17:9)

*And they kept silent and in those days told no one any of the
things they had seen.*

(Luke 9:36b)

Walking back down again can be a challenging experience. It
can be physically challenging, because the leg and foot

muscles are tired, and because everything is happening in reverse, with pressure points on the body opposite to where they were on the way up. It can be emotionally challenging, because the excitement of reaching the top now moves into facing what lies ahead. And it can be mentally challenging, because whatever took place at the summit somehow has to be digested and made sense of. Another spanner in the works is the extent to which vistas change: when I walk back down a hill, I see what I couldn't see on the way up, and notice things, whether it is sights far ahead or bushes nearby, in a new way. In other words, what seemed familiar now looks different. My perspectives on my world have changed.

Some of this lies in the background of the disciples' walk down the mountain. Life *has* changed. Nothing can be the same again. The change in Jesus' appearance, the sudden presence of Moses and Elijah, Peter's impulsive wish to 'freeze' the moment, the cloud and voice – all this must have provided the disciples with much to ponder. And if we add Matthew's depiction of Jesus approaching them, touching them, and telling them to rise up and not be afraid, we have a direct contact with Jesus, speaking to them about their state of mind, and reassuring them that something has indeed happened, but they're not to fear (Matt. 17:6–7). Seeing Jesus *alone* moves them suddenly back to some kind of normality, and yet it was not quite 'normal' any more, because what had happened did really happen.

I suppose that the question has to be asked at this point, 'what really did happen?' up there. Biblical scholars are sometimes reluctant to face this, partly because previous generations tended to take it at face value, and partly because the narratives are so rich in the kind of theological detail that we have been exploring, the variants in the evangelists' accounts, to say nothing of the richness of the interpreting tradition, whether that is to be found in the allegories of Jerome (Chapter 2), inspired by Origen, whom we shall be looking at shortly, or the more straight, expository style of

John Chrysostom (Chapter 5). A classic case of this caution is in any discussion of the kind of cloud that might have come and gone. It's not fanciful to speculate. Nor will it really do to say that the cloud is exclusively a theological motif, borrowed from the Old Testament.[2] Of course the Old Testament tradition of mountains and the cloud on Mount Sinai/Horeb must be the primal religious inspiration for the Transfiguration. But that might not be the whole story. My own view, for what it is worth, is that something did happen up there; and it may have happened more than once. Quite what *did* happen is hard to say in exact detail. But the fact that we have these three accounts, backed up by the additional 'witness' account (2 Pet. 1:16–19), suggests more than just a theological tradition. I have been sufficiently affected by hill-climbing with friends for me to realise at least the possibility that Jesus and his 'inner cabinet' went on a long trek, perhaps on more than one occasion, and that these special times apart, the climbing up and down included, made a significant impact on their sense of vocation and destiny. There might just be something geographical behind the theological truths we have been exploring.

That is why the vignette of the four of them descending in the Theophanes the Greek icon is so important. Like the other vignette on the left-hand side depicting their ascent, this one does not obtrude. It does not hit the onlooker in the face. After all, it is only an extra, a sideline on the main action. But it is there nonetheless, and the onlooker can see Jesus taking care of the other three, looking after them on their descent to the familiar world. One can even see that care expressed in the icon in both physical and spiritual terms. He is *helping* them walk down. But he is also *talking* with them. Unlike the other vignette, there is more than a suggestion of conversation. But whatever went into that conversation, whether it was initial or prolonged, Jesus' relationship with the other three remained critical. It was important that they made the most of what had taken place, however overwhelmed they were. And that is precisely the point: do we (they) ever get the message? What did they go on to do and be as Jesus' followers? Perhaps the other dimension that comes across is silence, because (according to Matthew and Mark) that is what is enjoined upon them by Jesus. Don't talk about it yet – because people won't understand, they won't be able to take it.

My own 'descent' from illness takes the form of con-valescence. I was 'chosen' for the illness, I 'ascended' for the treatment, I had my appearance 'changed' through the treat-ment, I wanted to 'hold' certain moments of it all – 'sacra-mental' moments that were sometimes far away from the Church's rituals – I then found it impossible (and useless) to do so, I wandered in a 'cloud of unknowing', I was aware of a voice speaking occasionally in my confusion and lack of faith, I 'saw' Jesus away from all the distractions because of the purging nature of the whole experience, and now I have to get used to normal life again. It is not easy. The routine of 'hos-pital time' that dominated my existence now has to adjust, so that 'normal time' and 'hospital time' now begin to compete. The experience can be very disorientating, because in a strange sort of way I have become dependent on the hospital, the nurses, the doctors, and look forward to my visits back, in order to see people who have helped to give my life back to me. 'Descending' to normal life takes time. Will I be able to cope with presiding at a public liturgy, when I've either been a patient in a sickbed with a chaplain visiting me, or I have been in my chapel with whichever members of the family, colleagues and friends have been around, isolated from the outside world because of the risk of infection?

The answer, of course, is yes. But I have become different. My world and my life have changed. My 'transfiguration' – in part a 'disfiguration' – has become part of me, and all that I can do about it is to take stock of it, try to make sense of it, realising that this may take some time. My 'descent' from the mountain, my convalescence from the illness, I know is described as 'remission', a word which has a curious extra theological tinge to it because my life has been 'remitted' to me. I don't know how long this will be, but the 'transfiguration/disfiguration' has resulted in my waking up every morning thankful to be alive in a way that has never been the case before. Modern medical science – and the prayers of many, many people – have meant that I *can* 'descend', and face the world. But it is a world that looks – and is – different for me now. There are parts of it that are much more attractive than they were before, just as there are parts of it that look unattractive, with one-issue Christians here, complaining letters there, and the rough and tumble of consumer religion.

There are many, many other forms of 'descent', silence – or even just reticence – being one ingredient of the process. And that is why the icon stands out as a kind of universal statement of what Transfiguration is. Writing in a foreword to a recent book on icons by Rowan Williams, Kallistos Ware puts it in a nutshell: '[Icons] help us to cross borders, to enter into a transfigured world.'[3] Here we see the genius of the whole notion of what it is to gaze upon an icon, as it helps us to pray our lives more fruitfully. The icon confronts us with the eternal truths of the Christian faith in such a way as to enable us to see our own lives somehow reflected in them. It is a superficial judgement to dismiss icons as fine works of art that paint a world that we simply cannot reach. If that were so, then there would be no point in looking at them. Theophanes the Greek seems determined to paint the disciples in as human terms as possible, with real doubts and fears – as is obvious from the posture and facial expressions of the three at the foot of the mountain, and the way that Jesus in those two vignettes leads them up and then takes them down again.

Other people's 'descents' are going to take millions of different forms, whether it is the sublime experience of a retreat in a religious house, the walk down the aisle at the end of a wedding, or variations on the more painful examples that I have drawn from my illness. To 'descend' again to the supposed 'real world', with all its fantasies, foibles and frettings, is an essential part of the life of faith. We can't dodge it. Peter tried – but failed – when he hit on the idea of building three tents, in order to shelter and contain the experience. So we are left to guess at what was going on in the minds of the disciples, and the flavours provided by the evangelists to that very question.

The three versions of the narrative deal with the descent in different ways, as we should by now come to expect. Mark and Matthew both say that Jesus actually told the disciples not to tell others about what had happened, whereas Luke gives an entirely different spin on the proceedings: the disciples have obviously decided themselves that they should not talk about it. Moreover, whereas Matthew has 'the vision' and Jesus' command is that they shouldn't speak about it until he has 'been raised', Mark is at once more reticent: 'what they had *seen*' and 'raised'. Matthew uses the technical word for a mystical vision, where Mark is more bald and allusive. Matthew then uses a more technical-sounding word (*egerthēi*), where Mark is more direct (*anastēi*).[4] Both these approaches one could say were 'in character'. Mark wants to avoid anything too explicit, since the disciples go on to miss the point. As Lee remarks, they had seen 'the source and certainty of salvation', but they don't grasp its true meaning. Equipped as they are for the journey that lies ahead, to Jerusalem and beyond, they won't begin to understand it until 'the Shepherd, having been struck, rises again to re-gather his scattered sheep'.[5] With Matthew, however, the context is different. Jesus tells them to be silent until they have all been commissioned from another mountain, and between then and now he must pass through the valley of the shadow of death.[6]

Both, however, agree that nothing must be said until after the resurrection. This is yet one more pointer to the fact that, whereas Moses and Elijah appeared in glory and one had died a natural death on earth and the other had been taken into heaven, Jesus must be *put to death*, and then *rise from the dead*.

The Transfiguration is not primarily about a good religious 'experience', whether of worship, prayer, meditation or whatever. It is about the harsh reality of an impending betrayal, trial, public crucifixion – and resurrection. The audience, the onlooker, participates in the unfolding drama because of its sweep from one event to another, living through them with the disciples, and knowing just how difficult it is to take full stock of every part of the proceedings and realise it for what it really means. Mark, as always, draws this out more sharply by his careful use of words, and by the way he suggests that it was all really beyond the disciples; and the same note is struck in their subsequent discussions, when they question the resurrection (Mark 9:10), wonder whether Elijah should not come first (Mark 9:11), and have to cope with the reality of the new Elijah really suffering (Mark 9:12–13). Matthew, on the other hand, has an eye for the final mountain at the end, where Jesus commissions them, promising his presence with them for ever (Matt. 28:26); Matthew's account of the ensuing conversation, concentrated on the difference between Jesus' fate and John the Baptist's (Matt. 17:10–13) is thus gentler on the disciples.

In both of them, too, Jesus 'commands' the disciples. He has said the same thing to the same three when Jairus's daughter was raised (Mark 5:37, 43); he also orders the crowd to say nothing after his miraculous healings (Mark 5:21–43; 7:31–37); and he tells the disciples to say nothing about Peter's confession that he is the Christ (Mark 8:30). Commands to silence have not, however, appeared in Matthew's gospel, except at the confession of Peter (Matt. 16:20). But we need to see Matthew's 'command' in the immediate context of what has just happened, Jesus telling the disciples to rise up and not to fear (Matt. 17:7).

With Luke, things are very different. It seems as if the disciples' tacit agreement not to say anything is an extension of Peter 'not knowing what he said' (Luke 9:33) when he wanted to build the three tents. The three of them, in other words, are reduced to complete silence – which is a different thing from Jesus telling them to be quiet about it. Moreover, this is something of a contrast from what happened earlier, when the disciples of John the Baptist came to quiz Jesus about what he was doing, and Jesus replied with the direct command that they should 'tell' John about it all (Luke 7:18– 22). A similar conclusion is to be drawn from the healing of the Gerasene demoniac, an incident that was published abroad, without any discouragement (Luke 8:34–39). Luke is happy for Jesus to let the world know what he is doing, but when it comes to the real meaning of his identity, that is different: when Peter confesses that Jesus is 'the Christ of God', Jesus tells the disciples not to say anything (Luke 9:21), and goes on to spell out what it means to be a disciple, which involves taking up one's cross daily in order to follow him (Luke 9:22–27). For Luke, there seems no need now for Jesus to instruct them to be silent about what they had seen. Indeed, as Lee suggests, Luke gives the disciples no tongues to speak of Jesus until the Spirit has come upon them (Luke 24:39; Acts 2:4), just as it came upon Jesus at his baptism (Luke 3:16–22).[7]

But what exactly did these three disciples go on to do? This is a question that is seldom asked in relation to the Transfiguration, but the answer reveals some interesting details in the different ways in which the evangelists portray them. Mark, with his tendency to be critical of the disciples, has James and John themselves coming up to ask Jesus for seats at his right and left hand in the Kingdom (Mark 10:35), which causes the remaining ten to be angry with them (Mark 10:41). Jesus nonetheless sticks with this unreliable and uncomprehending inner group when he takes them into Gethsemane (Mark 14:33), but they still join the remaining disciples and forsake him (Mark 14:50). Peter has a greater exposure in the gospel. But there is still the running theme of incomprehension: this occurs over such issues as the cost of discipleship (Mark 10:28), protesting that he won't desert Jesus (Mark 14:29), and the piquant scene in Gethsemane when Peter and the others fall asleep (Mark 14:37); all this reaches a climax when Peter denies Jesus three times after his arrest (Mark 14:54–72). Matthew follows a similar pattern, but it is less negative in overall tone. On the one hand, Mark uses the same word for 'leaving behind' when the disciples are first called by Jesus (Mark 1:18), which suggests that all is now lost, since they have now 'left' him (Mark 14:50). On the other hand, for Matthew all is this is to fulfil the purpose of God, as Jesus' words to the crowd at his arrest make clear (Matt. 26:56).

Different altogether is Luke's handling of the disciples. He does not include any reference to their forsaking Jesus, but goes straight to Peter following him at a distance (Luke 22:54), although he does include Peter's denial (Luke 22:56–62). As Raymond Brown remarks, 'he will not have them put in a bad light.'[8] So nuanced is Luke on them that he even includes an expression of fond hope that Jesus was indeed going to bring redemption to Israel – that is what the two disciples say to the stranger on the road to Emmaus (Luke 24:21). But Luke goes further, because in the Acts of the Apostles, Peter, James and John have prominent roles to fulfil as leaders of the new community. Peter is constantly referred to as the spokesman for the group, from the very start (Acts 1:15; 2:14, 37, 38). James is killed by Herod because of his position in the Jerusalem church (Acts 12:2). And John is depicted as a colleague of Peter, sharing his house (Acts 1:13), and working with him (Acts 3:1–4) in works of healing (Acts 3:11) and preaching (Acts 4:13). This is a different story altogether from that of Mark.

If we are to see the Transfiguration as a 'pivotal mandate', then the 'pivot' needs to move right forward into how those three men are depicted by the evangelists. For Mark, there is the underlying note of Jesus as an enigma. For Matthew, Jesus is the new Moses, fulfilling the Scriptures and the purposes of God. For Luke, Jesus is the saviour of the nations, taking history on into the life of the new community. This rebounds

on how the disciples are portrayed. But it is still the Transfiguration that is the pivot in each gospel. All three in their
different ways tell the same basic story of the remaking and
refashioning of humankind, which is perhaps most poign-
antly expressed in the portrayal of Peter in the gospel that
contains no Transfiguration narrative at all – the Fourth
Gospel. For here, Peter, who has denied Jesus (John 18:15–18,
25–27) is restored at the resurrection, a process that is not
immediate (John 20:16), but is eventual and real (John 21:1–
14), and ends with the threefold question, corresponding to
the threefold denial (John 21:15–19). In the last of the series of
homilies preached on John's gospel in 391 (the year after he
preached on Matthew), John Chrysostom comments in this
way on the restoration of Peter: 'Jesus asks him a third time,
and the third time gives him the same injunction, to show at
what a price he sets the care of his own sheep, and that this
especially is a sign of love towards him.'[9]

Among all the interpreters of the Bible in antiquity, one name
stands out, and that is Origen (*c.* 185–*c.* 254). Because of
political difficulties, he left behind a distinguished career in
his native Alexandria, where he had been head of the catechetical school and developed a reputation for his interpretation of the Bible, for Caesarea in Palestine. Here he
flourished even further, was ordained a presbyter, and
accepted from the bishops, who admired him, an invitation
to develop a preaching ministry, and he established what has
been described as the first Christian university. This caused
problems with his home church in Alexandria, which
regarded the ordination as uncanonical, and where only
bishops normally preached. Origen was already a controversial figure, and the tinge of controversy has never left
him. He was clear that the Bible could be interpreted in three
ways, the literal, the moral and the allegorical. It was the last
of these at which he excelled. He had a passion for placing
Christ at the centre of all his preaching, the Old Testament

138

included. This paved the way for many a future writer. His death was hastened by the torture he suffered at the instigation of the Roman governor during the time of the Emperor Decius.

Quite what lay at the heart of the stigma of Origen is not always clear, because so many of his works disappeared, and have to be read in Latin translation. Among other things, it was probably his teaching on the pre-existence of souls and his view that the resurrection body would be material. Although his works were condemned by the Emperor Justinian in 543, following a campaign by his detractors, Origen has benefited from some considerable rehabilitation in recent years. His strengths as a biblical expositor have been allowed to shine through and receive the appreciation they deserve. McGuckin even believes that it is Origen who is responsible for establishing Matthew's gospel as the main gospel of the Church's liturgical tradition.[10]

Origen's commentary on Matthew's gospel probably dates from 246–48. It is one of his most important works, coming from his maturity. It has come down to us in the original Greek, and he emerges from its pages as the first thoroughgoing allegorical interpreter.[11] Although it has gaps, his coverage of the Transfiguration narrative has survived in full. He acknowledges the tradition, obviously established in his time, that the verse of promise can be applied to the three chosen disciples, though he sidesteps wholly endorsing this view. Crucial for him is the theme of spiritual ascent, which is struck from the very beginning: 'He . . . transcends all the things of the world by beholding no longer the things which are seen.' The 'six days' refer to the creation, thus making this day, the day of Transfiguration, the new creation, for the one who will so ascend 'will keep a new Sabbath, rejoicing in the lofty mountain, because he sees Jesus transfigured before them' – and Origen places considerable emphasis on explaining the specific revelation implied by the words, 'before them'. Jesus is transfigured 'that he may be manifested to the children of light, who have put off the works of dark-ness' (Rom. 13:12). This leads him on to look at the garments of Christ, which 'are the expressions and letters of the gospels with which he invested himself'. In other words, the gospels are the *living* word of Christ, and part of that life means they need to be read liturgically and interpreted prayerfully and imaginatively. This brings him immediately face to face with Moses and Elijah, who are the Law and the Prophets. Origen is the first to take that specific view: 'If any one sees the glory of Moses, having understood the spiritual law as a discourse in harmony with Jesus, and the wisdom in the prophets which is hidden in a mystery, he sees Moses and Elijah in glory when he sees them with Jesus.' For Origen, the Old Testament is an essential part of the Christian Bible, and the two testaments belong to each other, which explains why he introduces Moses and Elijah a little earlier than the nar-rative allows.

Origen then deals with the garments of Jesus in their brightness, and again he returns to the business of biblical interpretation. Quoting Mark's reference to earthly bleachers (Mark 9:3), he takes a gentle side-swipe at 'wise men of this world who are careful about the phraseology which they consider to be bright and pure'. It is not altogether clear to whom he is referring, unless he means those who refuse to take that 'spiritual ascent' in their approach to preaching, those who are exclusively literal in their interpretation and who will admit of no allegorical dimension at all. We then come to Peter's interjection, which Origen takes to be a ploy in order to get Jesus to avoid the cross, and he parallels this with Peter's previous attempt (Matt. 16:23), when Jesus predicted his coming death. On this occasion, however, Peter is in a trance – a neat way of criticising him. This must have been an already established explanation: we find it in North Africa in the writings of Tertullian (*c.* 160–*c.* 225).[12] But another, less negative possibility is provided: perhaps Peter desires the contemplative life. When the cloud descends and the voice speaks, this could well be the Trinity, but again he holds back and suggests that Jesus is the bright cloud.

We now come to the descent, and it is here that Origen reveals himself yet again as an imaginative interpreter. Why should the disciples remain silent? Three reasons are offered. The first is that other people would not believe what they were told. The second is that they would be scandalised if they heard about this and then saw Jesus crucified: they would not be able to make sense of the connection between Transfiguration and Calvary. And third, referring back to what he has said earlier about Jesus' injunction to silence after Peter's confession (Matt. 16:20), silence is also necessary because of the very different kinds of people, with their different ways of understanding Jesus. Here we have the experienced teacher, for in the passage from his own writings to which he refers, Origen uses the process of catechetical instruction to illustrate how the words of Jesus need to be 'digested in the minds of the hearers, that, after there has been a period of silence in the proclamation of something of this kind about him, at a more reasonable time there might be built up upon the former rudiments "Christ Jesus crucified and raised from the dead"'.[13]

Origen's influence was far-reaching. His allegorical approach to Scripture long outlasted him, touching many others, including Jerome (see Chapter 2), who had an ambivalent relationship with his writings, thanks to the theological polemics of his time. He is the first to see the Trinity in the voice speaking about Jesus through the cloud, a view which others later took up. But it was not just allegory for which he is well known. He had a sharp eye on language, and was the first to suggest, in relation to the Lord's Prayer, that 'on earth as in heaven' should apply not just to the doing of the will, but to the two preceding petitions as well, hallowing the name and the coming of the Kingdom; this minority view kept recurring here and there, until 1888, when the Cambridge biblical scholars Westcott and Hort adopted it in their Greek text of the New Testament.[14] For Origen, scholarship and imagination go together.

The approach to the Transfiguration outlined here profoundly affected subsequent writings. Those three reasons offered to explain the command to silence, to reticence, reappear in different guises, not without variation, among later preachers and writers. The commentary by Ephrem (*c.* 303–373) on the *Diatessaron* makes much of this silence: people would not believe, they would be provoked to blasphemy, they must wait until they have received the power to speak of it (Acts 1:4), after the resurrection.[15] The language of being 'scandalised', which is not used by Origen, recurs in later writers, including Jerome and Bede, and found its way right through subsequent writers and preachers. But perhaps most unusual of all is what Gottfried of Admont (d. 1165) says in a Lenten sermon to his monks. Those who have been chosen to contemplate the sweetness of God should remain humble, and not seek any kind of human glory; they must therefore remain silent, until they rise to such a perfection that they are 'neither elevated by prosperity nor cast down by adversity'; and see the full and final vision of God.[16] Gottfried manages, perhaps unintentionally, to develop Origen's theme of 'spiritual ascent' in a way that reaches the needs of a monastic community. This is one more example of the significance of the great third-century exegete.

Many preachers overlook Jesus' words on the way down the mountain, perhaps because they have spent so much time on what has happened that they cannot see the importance of that process of 'digestion' which Origen rightly values. For all his brilliant handling of Scripture, and despite his (perhaps schematic) distinction between the 'simple' and the 'perfect' believer, Origen never loses sight of the importance of seeing the many different ways in which Jesus can relate to people, according to their needs, their gifts, their spiritual condition. Like all really great preachers, there is a sense, too, that he is fully aware of the sheer richness of Scripture. This leads him, for example, to his alternative suggestions about Peter's impulsive interjection (was it a ploy to stop the crucifixion, or perhaps was it born of a desire to contemplate Christ?), and about the meaning of the cloud and the voice (is this the Trinity, but, then, is Jesus the cloud?). We are treated to creative speculation, the work of the Holy Spirit in the imagination. But this is always seen in the context of Jesus, whose 'garments' are the gospels, lived and read and followed, and returned to yet again, as the community of faith prays through them in the liturgy and in life.

Icons are central to Eastern Christianity, and we in the West have learnt to love and to use them over the years as well. But the West is not lacking in its own artistic repertoire. For the Transfiguration, perhaps one of the most famous examples is the last painting of Raphael (Raffaello Sanzio), probably completed after his death in 1520.[17] Born in Urbino in 1483, the son of a painter, his short life was packed with fruitful encounters, which included Leonardo da Vinci and Michelangelo; and more than fourteen hundred works are attributed to him. The *Transfiguration* was commissioned by Cardinal Guilio de Medici (later to become Pope Clement VII) for his Cathedral in Narbonne in 1515, but it never reached there. Only a copy was sent, the original now being in the Vatican Pinacoteca. It is lush Renaissance, with a warm, powerful use of colour and perspective. There is a hint of the ascension in the Christ figure, and in addition to the three disciples lying in the centre, two further figures can be seen on the far left. But its uniqueness lies in the fact that, for some reason or another, Raphael has decided to include in the painting the first public action performed by Jesus after the Transfiguration – the healing of the epileptic boy, whom the disciples failed to heal by themselves. In Luke's gospel, this incident comes immediately, without any account of a discussion with the disciples (Luke 9:37–43), whereas Mark and Matthew recount it only after that conversation (Mark 9:14–29; Matt. 17:14–20). Mark's narrative of this healing is, surprisingly, the longest. Luke's is the shortest. And it is tempting to suggest that Raphael is following Luke in moving from the mountain immediately to the healing.

To the onlooker, this painting is an amazing mixture. The mountain-top action expresses the heavenly calling of Jesus, with Moses and Elijah on either side. There is a luminous cloud forming the background to Jesus, in the centre. The disciples draw us into this transformative event, which had been a universal feast of the Catholic Church for only about seventy years when Raphael began this work of art. But the healing of the epileptic boy in the lower part of the painting takes up just over half of the whole – and that is obvious straightaway. More to the point, whereas the upper scene is restricted to a small number of participants, the healing is crowded with people (as the gospels tell us), all of them – the lad most of all – astonished. The transfigured Lord, who appears only once, is not too high and mighty to heal an epileptic boy. The contrast is clear: Jesus is above, revealing himself to the disciples, but he is also putting right their failures below.

This combination of Transfiguration and healing is a good note on which to ponder the full implications of 'descent' from the mountain. It leaves us with questions to mull over about how we are to 'descend' to the world and fulfil our discipleship of Christ. When confronted with the 'voice of God', the question is 'who?', whereas the question posed of 'descent' is 'what now?' Anyone who has been through a unique experience, whether easy or difficult, will invariably think of the future, and what it will bring, and reticence while one mulls things over can be an essential virtue in a world that has so many words, spoken or written, broadcast or transmitted by other means, that we no longer seem able to trust them any more. A prayer in the 1978 American *Book of Lutheran Worship* strikes the right balance between our dependence on God and the uncertainty of a future that is – ultimately – in his transforming hands:

Lord God,
you have called your servants
to ventures of which we cannot see the ending,
by paths yet untrodden,
through perils unknown.
Give us faith to go out with courage,
not knowing where to go,
but only that your hand is leading us,
and your love supporting us;
through Jesus Christ our Lord.[18]

Chapter 10

DISCIPLESHIP TRANSFIGURED

The one who is transfigured on the mountain is the one who is disfigured by anguish, pain and death on the cross.

(Dorothy Lee)[1]

We did not follow cleverly devised myths when we made known to you the power and coming of our Lord Jesus Christ, but we had been eyewitnesses to his majesty. For he received honour and glory from God the Father when that voice was conveyed to him by the Majestic Glory, saying, 'This is my Son, my Beloved, with whom I am well pleased.' We ourselves heard this voice come from heaven, while we were with him on the holy mountain. So we have the prophetic message more fully confirmed. You will do well to be attentive to this as to a lamp shining in a dark place.

(2 Pet. 1:16–19)

Why did the Transfiguration happen? This is the question that lies behind any reading of the Scripture texts, any gaze at a colourful icon. By now, we have looked at the narratives in their varying detail and at some of the interpreters of these texts down the ages. We have considered the Transfiguration

146

in the light of human experience, easy or difficult. And in that connection, I am reminded of a poster that was once displayed outside a Danish university chaplaincy which said, 'If you haven't got any problems, come inside and we'll give you some!'

Again and again we have seen that Transfiguration hovers in the liturgical tradition, not quite sure of where it belongs. The tension between the August celebration (perhaps originating from a dedication festival for the church on Mount Tabor?) and the more basic Lenten observance is poignant. In one way it's good to have a festival in August in its own right, obliquely pointing to Holy Cross Day forty days later, but one wonders if people do get that point, and whether August is really the best time. The older tradition, in both East and West, of reading it in connection with Lent makes much more sense, connecting glory with cross, and preventing a 'stand-alone' existence, unconnected with Calvary and beyond. The exceptions, always easy to ignore in the interests of ironing out anomalies, are worth noticing. Hacket's Easter season[2] sermons in mid seventeenth-century London are the most extensive collection known on the Transfiguration; and Grundtvig's hymns and sermons for pre-Advent or late Epiphany in nineteenth-century Copenhagen offer extra dimensions that can easily be underestimated.

Moreover, we have been treated to interpretations that are at times directly expository (like that of John Chrysostom), allegorical (Jerome), mystical (Gregory Palamas), christological (Peter the Venerable), or ecclesiological (Mark Frank), and we are much the poorer for having failed to see the riches that are contained in these different approaches. We have seen, too, how impoverished the tradition has been in its almost exclusive use of Matthew's narrative, however often the preacher might glance at the other two. Mark and Luke have riches that are best seen by letting them speak for themselves, in order to benefit from attention to their own particular perspectives. This comes across when we consider Jerome's (unique) sermon on the Mark narrative; Luke fares rather better, with Ambrose of Milan's commentary, and the preaching of figures whom we have looked at in detail, such as John Hacket and Mark Frank in seventeenth-century England, as well as others whom we have brought into our discussion from time to time, such as Timothy in sixth-century Jerusalem. When these preachers and writers are set alongside modern biblical scholarship, whether it is Michael Ramsey's classic, or the work of John Paul Heil or Dorothy Lee, then we can see how much deeper and more penetrating the individual testimony of each evangelist can be when allowed to speak on his own.

Nor can each narrative be seen in isolation from its context. Whether it is Mark, or Matthew, or Luke, we have been able to view the Transfiguration within the overall approach of each gospel. This holds true whether it is Mark not men-tioning the face of Christ, when his portrait of Jesus is one of a persistent enigma, Matthew's depicting Jesus as the new Moses, teaching, healing, transfigured and commissioning disciples from mountains, or Luke's emphasis on the whole event taking place in the context of prayer – a recurring motif in his gospel. We have observed, too, how the earlier (Lenten) reading tended to include the verse of promise (Matt. 16:28), whereas the later (festal) reading tended to start with the ascent. Perhaps there is a case for reverting to that older custom. Rich as the modern liturgical lectionaries are in their careful attention to all three of these narratives, we might hope for yet more comprehensive provision in the prayers, eucharistic prefaces and, above all, hymnody, that are now available, in the best tradition of Peter the Venerable in the twelfth century. And there is surely scope for at least some of the writings we have looked at being made more accessible to contemporary readership.[3]

The heart of Transfiguration is that it needs to be seen both as an *event* and as a *process*. That is why John Paul Heil is on target with his repeated suggestion that on the mountain, we the 'audience' are given a 'pivotal mandate', to look back to what Jesus has said and done already, and then look forward to what is to come. The Transfiguration, as Michael Ramsey suggested years ago, is indeed 'a gateway to the saving events of the Gospel'.[4] This is why, for example, it becomes such a quarry for understanding both the person and work of Christ, obvious in the context, as well as the doctrine of the Trinity, first explored by Origen in the third century, and then by Jerome at the end of the fourth, and taken up in the West by Bede in the eighth, but not developed in the East until later. All this spills out into the way we think about the life of discipleship, for if we are looking for a 'result' of the Transfiguration, it is about the way we follow Christ.

First of all, the Transfiguration is about the tension between continuity and discontinuity.[5] Time and again, this is referred to by preachers and writers when we look at Moses and Elijah, as well as the disciples on their way down the mountain – and how they manage (or fail to manage) to get the message in their subsequent following of Jesus. So far from being a wooden exercise that is once given and that is the end of it, the Transfiguration concerns how the faith is revealed, and the extent to which life as we experience it will always have something of the mixture of continuity and discontinuity. The familiar figures, Moses and Elijah, find themselves enveloped in a cloud. This is not to suggest that any common point of reference will do. But what it does suggest is that the life of faith means living with points of old arrival and stages of new departure – the true 'exodus' that is risky, unknown, yet centred on the cross. Transfiguration 'baptises' incipient faith.

Then we come to the way the disciples are changed by this grace-filled encounter. The Transfiguration is not a spiritual luxury with a feel-good factor. It is Christ-centred and therefore concerns the Church's discipleship. It concerns the understandably human desire to stay and enjoy the heights of revelation and prolong them as much as possible, thereby turning them into a human construct. But once again, we are

reminded of its true purpose. We are a community of faith
journeying towards the cross. As F. D. Maurice (1805–72) puts
it: 'Visible insignificance accompanied invisible energy.'[6] That
cloud both conceals and envelops, and when removed leaves
those gazing at the spectacle with both a sense of hiddenness
and a sense of mobility. The sheer fact of God in Trinity, the
Father in the voice, the Spirit in the cloud, manifesting the
transfigured Christ, points to the essential distance between
humankind and the deity – a distance breached by Jesus, to
whom we alone must attend. No wonder Gregory Palamas
was so insistent that whatever inkling we have of God's presence, this is a gift to us, in prayer, not a human attainment,
not the result of what he calls 'a sensory and created power'.

What does the Transfiguration say to the Church today? It
speaks of continuity and discontinuity as the stuff of the
development of doctrine – and the role of conflict in that
process. We have not been looking at great theological think-
ers in ivory towers across the centuries. Some of them were
misunderstood in their own time (like Origen), some had to
withstand opposition to their scholarship (like Jerome in his
determination to produce the first really accurate Latin Bible –
not a popular quest!), others had to fight battles about the
place of the Transfiguration in the life of prayer (like Gregory
Palamas), while others again were either a mite too big for
their own contemporaries (like Grundtvig) or working hard at
achieving a theological balance at a time when religious faith
had become polarised both politically and theologically (like
Hacket). And whether we are Easterners, basking in one of
the long-established 'Twelve Feasts', or Westerners, 'reading'
it as a minor festival in August or a narrative that is an
essential ingredient of Lent, its resources remain as rich and
varied as ever. All this means being open to new ways of
being a Christian, where worship and discipleship are not
lived in separate compartments, but where the one flows out
of the other, and the cross is central as the ultimate source of
change both in form and in being. It speaks, too, of the need to

listen to the voice that can, in spite of everything, penetrate not only its own 'cloud of unknowing' but our own (at times) thick skulls, recalling us to be part of a Church whose response must be to look askance at even the most impressive structures and the most transparent processes.

If I learnt one thing about being in hospital for so long, it is that I rejoiced in being bathed by the prayer of the Church, offered in many places and by many people, but I was living beyond the edge of its sometimes narrow perspectives. For me, the 'transfiguration' of my 'disfiguration' during chemotherapy involved quasi-sacramental moments that would be hard to describe, but that simply 'happened'. Of course there is an 'and yet' about the humanity of the Christian community, with all its limitations and narrowness; the Transfiguration hints at how the disciples failed to get the message, especially in Mark's gospel. But limitations and narrowness are not the prerequisite of the community of faith: the big, wide world has its own horrific memories, such as the atomic bombing of Hiroshima on 6 August 1945. This provoked the following words from Kenneth Leech in a sermon on the fiftieth anniversary in St Anne's Church, Manchester: 'Transfiguration can and does occur "just round the corner", occurs in the midst of perplexity, imperfection, and disastrous misunderstanding.'[7]

Transfiguration pulls us out of the mire of our ordinariness, and the sheer weight and depth of some of the preaching and writing we have looked at is a sobering reminder of what this can entail. It does, therefore, mean looking again at the subtle interaction of the mountain-top experience and the plodding walk of faith across the plain of dull, everyday life. What Luz describes as the 'chiastic' structure,[8] of ascent and descent, Jesus with Moses and Elijah and then alone, places the cloud and the voice at the dramatic summit; and this forms a pattern of discipleship both mystified and illuminated by the un-created light of God himself. Today's Church too easily drives a wedge between self-conscious religious experience, which somehow has to be lived on some kind of contrived 'high', and a discipleship for which, in real daily terms, the followers of Jesus are sometimes ill equipped. Like an icon with inverted perspectives and the capacity to draw me into a different way of looking at both time and eternity, the Transfiguration enables me to see everything in my life in a new and different way altogether.

Discipleship is just as much about the ordinary, trudging walk of faith as it is about moments of disclosure which are spelt out, not in terms of unrestrained hyperbole, but in the material of our experience, mountains, clouds, voices and familiar points of reference, which are for a moment trans-formed by a new coherence, a fresh 'reading' of Scripture. Our pilgrimage is fed on visions, words and sacraments that are themselves reinterpretations of our own lives, our own experiences, our own familiar tools of communication – silence included. And, at their highest and deepest, they 'root' us in that heavenly, cross-centred 'detachment' which has the power to shake us out of our complacency, our tired stereo-types, our prejudices, and our masks of self-deception. Transfiguration is not about living in a religious ghetto. Peter's crass suggestion, and what followed thereafter, the descent included, give us ample evidence to the contrary. It is, rather, about pointing us to a new life in Christ that is always to come, the transformation of our common culture. Pope Callixtus III's context, of using the defeat of the Turks at Belgrade in 1456 somehow as a statement of Christian superiority, is enough of a warning of the importance of inter-faith dialogue, of using what we have in common – mountains, Moses and Elijah, and the search for the mystery of God – as starting points along the road to better under-standing, despite all the differences that persist between the three Abrahamic faiths.

Transfiguration is both an event and a process. To live the Transfiguration to the full is not possible in the world as we know it, where knowledge is by its very nature only partial. Compared with the our gospel-writers, the author of 2 Peter provides only a partial account, which does not mention Moses and Elijah, the fear of the disciples, or even the cloud.[9] But like him, we are still 'eyewitnesses', although in another way: we are with Jesus on the mountain every time we read that narrative, pray that narrative, live that narrative. 'Eye-witness' is an important biblical word, with Old Testament resonances on what two or three witnesses can do to verify truth (Deut. 17:6). To hear is one thing, to see it is another. As the Fourth Gospel, noticeably lacking the narrative altogether, yet permeated with Transfiguration from beginning to end, makes clear right at the start, 'we have seen his glory' (John 1:14), a text frequently referred to in Transfiguration sermons. That is why the early Christians set such store by the need to hand on the apostolic witness, and not leave it to gather dust. We may not put it all into exactly the right words, but to 'see' the true meaning of one's life, to 'see' it in a new 'light', is a transfiguring moment, in a world where women and men together not only form the apostolic band of disciples but are more and more included in the ministries of the Church.[10]

Rowan Williams has recently observed that 'art always approaches the condition of being both recognition and transmission of gift, gratuity or excess: but it always *approaches*.'[11] On that reckoning, art by its very creativity suggests and evokes and at the same time challenges and invites. Like the icon by Theophanes the Greek, the repertoire of Transfiguration themes is almost too full: God as unknown, spiritual vision, spiritual ascent, the epiphany of Christ as Son of God, the revelation of the inner life of God in Trinity, the prelude to the passion, the unity of the Old and the New Covenants, our redemption in sharing the life of God, the Resurrection, a foretaste of the completion of all things on the Last Day.[12] At the human end, the demands are equally varied. The promise at the start requires faith; the ascent turns that faith into risk; the change in appearance makes faith realise its need of receptiveness; our sudden enthusiasm ends up giving us courage, even to want to do the wrong thing; the cloud fills us with different sorts of fear, characterising the need for endurance; the voice is about love, not just for the 'beloved' Son, but for us; and the descent can only be about hope. None of these are pre-packed 'conditions' that we can somehow 'meet' or, if we don't, hold God to ransom. They are, rather, signposts on a journey, provided by Jesus, just as the waters of baptism and the eucharistic bread and wine and the oil of healing are transfigured along the way.

The Transfiguration can easily be swept away, if not as a marginal episode contained only in three gospels, then (more seriously) as no more than a human construct, no more than a requirement for those whose genetic formation somehow makes them naturally religious. Yet the array of preachers we have been looking at shows us that the Transfiguration not only meets every human condition, but 'clarifies it'; and here one slightly envies Grundtvig in having a language in which that word *forklarelse* is in everyday usage, and not a technical-sounding term like 'transfigure'. It is its own 'pivot' in the gospel of salvation, beckoning us back into the teaching of Christ and forward to his death and resurrection. In other words, it is about *God*, and the Gospel. Even atheists like Lewis Wolpert see the need for religious people 'to give comfort and meaning to their life'; and he observes that 'the loss of religious belief could have very serious consequences, and so could the enforcement of those beliefs on others'.[13] But we are not talking here just of 'comfort and meaning', as if the faith were an individual therapy, nor am I trying to 'enforce' my belief on others, in an act of theological imperialism. My genetic make-up may incline me in certain directions, whether it is the music I like or the food I enjoy, or even towards particular forms of religious art and numinous architecture. But for the life of faith I need a community of diverse people with quite different temperaments and views, to challenge and enrich me, to nurture and sustain me, to pray for me, especially when I particularly need it – which, when all is said and done, is another way of saying that faith is not a solo exercise, as the disciples discovered on the mountain.

Contemporary literature, however, is as full of fiction as it is of aggressive critique of religious faith. J. K. Rowling strikes an amusing note when Harry Potter, at the Hogwarts School of Witchcraft and Wizardry, sits under Professor McGonagall for lessons in Transfiguration. Yet we never learn what these are really about (or so it appears), only that it is 'complex and dangerous', and anyone 'messing around . . . will leave and not come back'![14] Even in such a world of 'real' make-believe as this, it would seem that there have to be some boundaries that cannot be transgressed. The Transfiguration of Jesus, however, may be 'complex' but it is not 'dangerous', in the sense of being a magician's trick with potentially nasty consequences. There are, however, plenty of borders that are shifted as we enter more and more into a mystery that is far from being what the author of 2 Peter refers to as 'cleverly devised myths'. When I look at the many motifs thrown up by tradition, three in particular stand out: Origen's image of Christ wearing those garments as the Scripture is interpreted in the Church; Grundtvig's grasp of the contemporaneity of the Transfiguration in the life of that community here and now, in spite of the distance in time; and John Chrysostom's moral challenge to *live* the faith.

The Scriptures do indeed need to be 'read' in new and fresh ways, so that the Gospel can be lived, and the songs of the mountain-top experience keep being sung in worlds apparently far removed from Mount Tabor but every bit as much a part of its all-embracing, all-enveloping cloud of uncreated light. Two very different people provide a fitting conclusion to our explorations, both of them hymn-writers. The first is from a hymn written for Great Vespers for the Transfiguration in the Byzantine rite by Cosmas Melodus (*c.* 675–751), a monk who became a bishop near Gaza, and who composed many hymns still sung today.

Before Thy Crucifixion, O Lord, the mountain became as
heaven and a cloud spread itself out to form a tabernacle.
When Thou wast transfigured and the Father testified
unto Thee, Peter with James and John were there, who
were to be present with Thee also at the time of Thy
betrayal; that, having beheld Thy wonders, they should
not be afraid before Thy suffering. Grant in Thy great
mercy that we too may be counted worthy to venerate
these Thy sufferings in peace.

Before Thy crucifixion, O Lord, taking the disciples up
into a high mountain, Thou wast transfigured before
them, shining upon them with the bright beams of Thy
power: from love of mankind and in Thy sovereign
might, Thy desire it was to show them the splendour of
the Resurrection. Grant that we too in peace may be
counted worthy of this splendour, O God, for Thou art
merciful and lovest mankind.[15]

Cosmas basks in the *annual* celebration of the feast. Charles
Wesley (1701–88), perhaps the greatest hymn-writer produced by the English-speaking world, encapsulates the *daily*
appropriation of the transfigured saviour:

> Christ, whose glory fills the skies,
>   Christ the true, the only light,
> Sun of righteousness, arise,
>   Triumph o'er the shades of night;
> Dayspring from on high, be near;
> Daystar in my heart appear.
>
> Dark and cheerless is the morn
>   Unaccompanied by thee;
> Joyless is the day's return,
>   Till thy mercy's beams I see,
> Till they inward light impart,
> Glad my eyes, and warm my heart.

Visit then this soul of mine,
　Pierce the gloom of sin and grief;
Fill me, radiancy divine,
　Scatter all my unbelief;
More and more thyself display,
Shining to the perfect day.[16]

This is why Jesus was transfigured – for us, and for our salvation.

NOTES

CHAPTER 1: ICON AS NARRATIVE

1. A. M. Ramsey, *The Glory of God and the Transfiguration of Christ* (London: Longmans, 1949, 2nd edn Libra Books, 1967), p. 145.

2. See Andreas Andreopoulos, *Metamorphosis: The Transfiguration in Byzantine Theology and Iconography* (Crestwood NY: St Vladimir's Seminary Press, 2005), pp. 244–50; see also figure 22a for colour reproduction. This is an excellent study; but his attribution to Ephrem the Syrian of a Greek homily probably preached in Antioch two or three centuries later (pp. 73, 85, 219) needs to be noted, see below, n.20, Sachot, p. 442.; see also Ch. 5 n. 19.

3. See, for example, W. D. Davies and Dale C. Allison Jr, *The Gospel According to St Matthew* Vol. II, Critical and Exegetical Commentary Series (Edinburgh: T&T Clark, 1988), pp. 668–718; Edward Schweizer, *The Good News According to Mark* (London: SPCK, 1970), pp. 180–3; and C. F. Evans, *Saint Luke*, TPI New Testament Commentaries (London: SCM Press/Philadelphia: Trinity Press, 1990), pp. 413–21.

4. John Paul Heil, *The Transfiguration of Jesus: Narrative Meaning and Function of Mark 9:2–8, Matt. 17:1–8 and Luke 9:28–36*, Analecta Biblica 144 (Roma: Editrice Pontificio Istituto Biblico, 2000).

5. Dorothy Lee, *Transfiguration*, New Century Theology (London/New York: Continuum, 2004); see also the important work of Harald Riesenfeld, *Jésu Transfiguré: L'arrière-plan du récit évangélique de la transfiguration de notre-seigneur*, Acta Seminarii Neotestamentico Upsaliensis XVI (København: Munksgaard, 1947), esp. on the central 'motifs', pp. 243–64.

6. See in particular Ulrich Luz, *Matthew 8—20: A Commentary*, tr. James E. Crouch (Minneapolis: Fortress Press, 1990), pp. 393–404.

7. John Anthony McGuckin, *The Transfiguration of Christ in Scripture and Tradition*, Studies in the Bible and Early Christianity 9 (Lewiston/Queenston: Edwin Mellen Press, 1986).

8. Lee, *Transfiguration*, p. 11; see also 'Mark, Memory and Gospel', a

158

paper by Martin Kitchen, read to the British New Testament Conference, Edinburgh, September 2004.

9. *Sermons Preached in Salisbury Cathedral Church and Elsewhere by John Wordsworth* (London: Longmans, 1913), pp. 277, 278 (whole sermon, pp. 277–84; for 'dear sons, members of our Theological College', p. 282).

10. Texts in Migne, *Patrologia Latina* 92.80–1 (Matthew), 245–50 (Mark), and 453–6 (Luke).

11. Graham N. Stanton, *A Gospel for a New People: Studies in Matthew's Gospel* (Edinburgh: T&T Clark, 1990).

12. Lee, *Transfiguration*, p. 59.

13. Hans Conzelmann, *The Theology of Saint Luke* (London: Faber and Faber, 1960). The German title is *Die Mitte Der Zeit* ('The Middle of the Age').

14. For Ambrose, *Expositio Evangelii Secundam Lucam* VII.6–20, see Gabriel Tissot (ed.), *Ambroise de Milan: Sur S. Luc I*, Sources Chrétiennes I bis (Paris: Éditions du Cerf, 1971), pp. 10–16; for Cyril of Alexandria, *Homily 51*, see R. M. Tonneau (ed.), *S. Cyrilli Alexandrini Commentarii in Lucam: Pars Prior*, Corpus Scriptorum Christianorum Orientalium 140: Scriptores Syri 70 (Louvain: Dubecq, 1953), pp. 119–22; for Proclus, *Oration VIII*, see Migne, *Patrologia Graeca* 65.763–72; ET in McGuckin, *The Transfiguration of Christ in Scripture and Tradition*, pp. 182–7; for Timothy of Jerusalem, *In Crucem et in Transfigurationem*, see Migne, *Patrologia Graeca* 86.255–66.

15. Heil, *Transfiguration of Jesus*, p. 319.

16. See Ramsey, *The Glory of God and the Transfiguration of Christ*, pp. 57–81.

17. Lee, *Transfiguration*, pp. 100ff.

18. Lee, *Transfiguration*, pp. 88ff.

19. See Leo the Great, *Sermon* 51 in René Dolle OSB (ed.), *Léon le Grand: Sermons 38–64*, Sources Chrétiennes 74 (Paris: Éditions du Cerf, 1961), pp. 14–21; and in *The Nicene and Post-Nicene Fathers*, Second Series, Vol. XII (Edinburgh: T&T Clark, 1989), pp. 162–5; for Chrysostom, see Ch. 5 nn. 1 and 14.

20. See Roselyne de Féraudy, 'Origine de la celebration de la Transfiguration' in *L'Icône de la Transfiguration*, Spiritualité Orientale 23 (Bégrolle: Abbaye de Bellefontaine, 1978), pp. 113–16; Jean Tomajean, 'La Fête de la Transfiguration (6 Août)', *L'Orient Syrien* 5 (1960), pp. 479–82; and Maurice Sachot, *L'homélie pseudochryostomienne sur la transfiguration CPG 4724, BHG 1975: Contextes liturgiques, Restitution à Léonce, prêtre de Constantinople, Édition critique et commentée, Traduction et etudes connexes*, Publications Universitaires Européennes: Série XXIII (Frankfurt am Main/Bern: Peter D. Lang, 1981), pp. 22–35 (pp. 33–5 for identification with Andrew of Crete).

21. See Andreopoulos, *Metamorphosis*, pp. 127ff.

22. See R. W. Pfaff, *New Liturgical Feasts in Later Medieval England* (Oxford: Clarendon Press, 1970), pp. 13ff.; for Peter the Venerable, see Ch. 8.

23. See Andreopoulos, *Metamorphosis*, p. 65.

CHAPTER 2: PROMISE

1. Jerome, *Epistle* 46.13 (to Marcella) in *Nicene and Post-Nicene Fathers*, Second Series, Vol. VI (Edinburgh; T&T Clark, 1996), p. 65; cf. *Epistle* 108.13, p. 202, written to Eustochium on the death of Paula, her mother: 'She made the ascent of Mount Tabor whereon the Lord was transfigured. In the distance she beheld the range of Hermon.'

2. Andreopoulos, *Metamorphosis*, pp. 244ff.

3. Evans, *Saint Luke*, p. 412.

4. H. B. Swete, *The Gospel According to St Mark* (London: Macmillan, 1908), p. 186.

5. Text in Migne, *Patrologia Graeca* 89.1361–76.

6. For text of *Diatessaron* (Sec. 24), see *The Ante-Nicene Fathers* (Edinburgh: T&T Clark, 1995), p. 80; for Ephrem, *Commentary on Diatessaron* XIV.5–12, see Louis Leloir (ed.), *Éphrem de Nisibe: Commentaire sur l'Évangile concordant ou Diatessaron*, Sources Chrétiennes 121 (Paris: Cerf, 1966), pp. 244ff.

7. For John Chrysostom, *Hom. In Matt.* 56.3, see Chapter 5 nn. 1 and 14; for Cyril of Alexandria, *Homilia 51 in Lucam*, see Tonneau, *S. Cyrilli Alexandrini Commentarii in Lucam*, p. 119; for Hilary of Poitiers, *In Matthaeum* 17:1–4, see J. Doignon (ed.), *Hilaire de Poitiers: Sur Matthieu II*, Sources Chrétiennes 258 (Paris: Cerf, 1969), pp. 60–3 (Hilary treats this verse as Matt. 17:1); for Augustine, *Sermon 78* see Edmund Hill (tr.), *The Works of St. Augustine: Sermons III/3* (New York: New City Press, 1991), p. 340; for Jerome, see below, nn. 11–14. See also Andrew Louth's discussion in 'St Augustine's interpretation of the Transfiguration of Christ', *Studia Ephemeridis Augustinianum* 68 (2000), pp. 375–82, where he compares Augustine with Origen, Ambrose and Jerome (though not Hilary).

8. See Pfaff, *New Liturgical Feasts*, p. 19: on the feast in the West, see on Peter the Venerable, Chapter 8.

9. Swete, *The Gospel According to St Mark*, pp. 185–6.

10. See J. N. D. Kelly, *Jerome* (London: Duckworth, 1975), esp. pp. 222–5.

11. Jerome, *Homily 80* in Sister Marie Liguori Ewald IHM (tr.), *The Homilies of St Jerome II*, Fathers of the Church 57 (Washington DC: Catholic University of America Press, 1965), pp. 159–68; Latin text in G. Morin (ed.), *S. Hieronymi Presbyteri: Tractatus Sive Homiliae in*

Psalmos, in Marci Evangelium aliaque varia Argumenta, Corpus Christianorum Series Latina 78 (Turnhout: Brepols, 1958), pp. 477–84; see also Jean-Louis Gourdain, 'Jérôme, Evégète de la Transfiguration, *Revue des Études Augustiniennes* 40 (1994), pp.365–73.

12. Cf. *Hebrew Names* in Migne, *Patrologia Latina* 23.825.
13. See Émille Bonnard (ed.), *Jérome: Commentaire sur S. Matthieu II*, Sources Chrétiennes 249 (Paris: Cerf, 1979), pp. 26–35.
14. See Ewald (tr.), *The Homilies of St. Jerome II*, p. 149; Latin text in Morin, *S. Hieronymi Presbyteris Tractatus*, p. 471; quoted in full in Thomas C. Oden and Christopher A. Hall (eds), *Ancient Commentary on Scripture Series: New Testament II: Mark* (Downers Grove IL: Inter-Varsity Press, 1998), p. 76.
15. For Bede, *Homily* 1.24, in Lawrence T. Martin and David Hurst OSB (tr.), *Bede the Venerable: Homilies on the Gospels I: Advent to Lent*, Cistercian Studies Series 110 (Kalamazoo MI: Cistercian Publications, 1990), pp. 234–44; it also begins at Matt. 16:27; perhaps not actually delivered as a sermon, it was nonetheless prepared for use in Lent. For the commentaries, see Migne, *Patrologia Latina* 92.80–1 (Matthew), 215–20 (Mark), 453–6 (Luke).
16. Jerome, *Epistle* 29 in *Nicene and Post-Nicene Fathers*, Second Series, Vol. VI, p. 439.
17. See John Wilkinson, *Jerusalem Pilgrims Before the Crusades* (Warminster: Aris and Phillips, 2002), p. 356.
18. Mechtild of Magdeburg, *Revelations: The Flowing Light of the Godhead* V, 30, tr. Lucy Menzies in *Mechtild of Magdeburg: Revelations: The Flowing Light of the Godhead* (London: Longmans, 1953), V, 30, pp. 122–3; translation adapted by Robert Atwell in *Celebrating the Seasons* (Norwich: Canterbury Press, 1999), pp. 132–3.

CHAPTER 3: ASCENT

1. See Thomas Plume (ed.), *A Century of Sermons upon several remarkable subjects preached by the Right Revd Father in God John Hacket, late Lord Bishop of Lichfield and Coventry* (London: Andrew Clark, 1675), p. 415.
2. See Davies and Dale Allison, *The Gospel According to St Matthew*, p. 694.
3. John C. Poirier, 'Jewish and Christian Tradition in the Transfiguration', *Revue Bénédictine* 111.4 (2004), pp. 516–30, argues that the narrative owes more to late Jewish speculation about Elijah and the coming Messiah.
4. Suggested by Swete, *The Gospel According to St Mark*, p. 187.
5. See Kenneth Stevenson, *All The Company of Heaven: A Companion to the Principal Festivals of the Christian Year* (Norwich: Canterbury

Press, 1998), pp. 24–7 (Conversion of St Paul), 28–31 (Presentation in the Temple), 38–41 (Annunciation), 54–6 (Matthias), 57–60 (Visitation), 64–7 (Birth of John the Baptist), 131–6 (Stephen), 174–6 (Ascension), 177–80 (Pentecost).

6. Andreopoulos, *Metamorphosis*, *passim*.
7. Heil, *The Transfiguration of Jesus*, p. 152; cf. Riesenfeld, *Jésu Transfiguré*, pp. 217–22.
8. Ambrose, *Expositio Evangelii Secundam Lucam* VII, 6–7 in Tissot, *Ambroise de Milan: Sur S. Luc I*, pp. 10–12; Hilary of Poitiers is known to have influenced him, in his Commentary on St Matthew, the first such to have survived, see *In Matthaeum* 17.2 in Doignon, *Hilaire de Poitiers: Sur Matthieu II*, pp. 62–3.
9. Evans, *Saint Luke*, p. 415.
10. Lee, *Transfiguration*, p. 65.
11. Text in A. Guillou, 'Le monastère de la Théotokos au Sinaï', *Mélanges d'archéologie et d'histoire* 67 (1955), pp. 237–57 (whole article, pp. 217–58).
12. Heil, *The Transfiguration of Christ*, pp. 202–3 (cf. pp. 152–3 on Mark).
13. Leo the Great, *Sermon* 51.2 in Dolle, *Léon le Grand*, p. 17; and *Nicene and Post-Nicene Fathers*, Second Series, Vol. XII, p. 163.
14. Augustine, *Sermon* 78.3, and *Sermon* 79A.2 in Hill, *The Works of St. Augustine: Sermons III/3*, pp. 341, 348.
15. John Chrysostom, *Hom. in Matt.* 56.6, *Nicene and Post-Nicene Fathers*, First Series, Vol. X, p. 348.
16. See memoir of his life by Plume, in *A Century of Sermons*, pp. i–liv; see also Kenneth Stevenson ' "In all supernatural works we rather draw back than help on": The Seven Transfiguration Sermons of John Hackett (1592–1670)', forthcoming in Natalie K. Watson and Stephen Burns (eds.), *Exchanges of Grace: Essays in Honour of Ann Loades* (London: SCM, 2008).
17. Plume, *A Century of Sermons*, pp. 411–79.
18. Plume, *A Century of Sermons*, p. 411.
19. Plume, *A Century of Sermons*, p. 456.
20. Plume, *A Century of Sermons*, pp. 411–21.
21. Bernard of Clairvaux: ref. Hacket, p. 414: Hacket's margin-note reads, '*In Ascens. Dom. Sermon 4*', and he quotes directly from the sermon: '*non solum meditemur in praemiis, sed etiam in mandatis Domini*' ('let us meditate not only on the rewards, but also on the commands of the Lord'); for the whole sermon, see Jean Leclercq OSB and H. Rochais (eds), *S. Bernardi Opera* Vol. V: *Sermones II* (Romae: Editiones Cistercienses, 1968), pp. 137–48; for this quotation, see p. 146 (*In Ascensu Domini Sermo* IV.10); Bernard, whose Christology is strongly affected by the Ascension, preached no fewer than six

sermons on this festival, this particular one centring on mountains and their place in the life and teaching of Christ. On the non-inclusion of Andrew, cf. Paschasius Radbertus (c. 790–c. 860), *Expositio in Matthaeum* VIII.xvii, Migne, *Patrologia Latina* 120.578, whom Hacket read but does not cite here.

22. cf. 'the Father in the voice, the Son in the flood, the Holy Ghost in the shape of a dove' and 'the Son in the water, the Holy Ghost in the dove, the Father in the voice', from the 1612 and 1615 Whitsun sermons, for which see *The Sermons of Lancelot Andrewes*, Library of Anglo-Catholic Theology (Oxford: Parker, 1841), pp. 188, 675.

23. For Ephrem, *Commentary on Diatessaron* XIV.12 in Leloir, *Éphrem de Nisibe: Commentaire*, p.249; for Proclus, *Oratio VIII* in Migne, *Patrologia Graeca* 65.765–6; for Anastasius of Antioch, *Sermo I* in Migne, *Patrologia Graeca* 89.1367–8; for John of Damascus, *Homilia de Transfiguratione* in Migne, *Patrologia Graeca* 96.545–76; ET in McGuckin, *The Transfiguration of Christ in Scripture and Tradition*, pp. 205–25.

24. Plume, *A Century of Sermons*, p. 426.

25. Text in Frank Colquhoun, *Parish Prayers* (London: Hodder and Stoughton, 1967), p. 387.

CHAPTER 4: CHANGE

1. See below n. 17, *Grundtvigs Sangværk* Vol. IV No. 250, p. 323; this is the first stanza of the best-known of Grundtvig's Transfiguration hymns; see *Den Danske Salmebog* (København: De Kgl, Vajsenhus' Forlag, 2003), No. 161, p. 181.

2. George Steiner, *Real Presences* (London: Faber and Faber, 1989), p. 226.

3. See, for example, Andreopoulos, *Metamorphosis*, pp. 23–36.

4. Leo the Great, *Homily* 51.6, in Dolle, *Léon le Grand: Sermons 38–64*, p. 20.

5. Leo the Great, *Homily* 51.5, in Dolle, *Léon le Grand*, p. 19.

6. Heil, *The Transfiguration of Jesus*, p. 156; see also Heil's discussion of the face and clothes of Jesus, pp. 80–92.

7. Swete, *The Gospel According to St Mark*, p. 188.

8. Lee, *Transfiguration*, p. 17.

9. Lee, *Transfiguration*, p. 46; cf. Riesenfeld, *Jésu Transfiguré*, pp. 97–129.

10. Heil, *The Transfiguration of Jesus*, p. 205.

11. Heil, *The Transfiguration of Jesus*, p. 260.

12. Origen, *Commentary on Matthew* XII.38, see Ch. 9 n. 11; Ambrose, *Expositio Evangelii secundam Lucam* VII.13 in Tissot (éd), *Ambroise de*

Milan: Sur S. Luc I, p. 13; Augustine, *Sermon* 78.2 in Hill (tr.), *The Works of St Augustine: Sermons* III/3, p. 340.

13. See Bede, *Homily* 1.24, in Martin and Hurst, *Bede the Venerable: Homilies on the Gospels I*, p. 238; Anselm, *Homilia* 4 in *Patrologia Latina* 158.605; Peter of Blois, *De Transfiguratione Domini* in *Patrologia Latina* 207.780.

14. See *Thomas Kingos Graduale* (Odense: Schrøder, 1699; reprinted Odense: Andelsbogtrykkeriet, 1967), pp. 117–18 ('Om Himmeriges Rige').

15. The main study on Grundtvig in English is A. M. Allchin, *N. F. S. Grundtvig: An Introduction to His Life and Work* (London: Darton, Longman and Todd, 1997); Danish tr. *Grundtvigs Kristendom: Menneskeliv og Gudstjeneste* (Aarhus: Universitetsforlag, 2002); see also Christian Thodberg and Anders Pontoppidan Thyssen (eds), *N. F. S. Grundtvig: Tradition and Renewal* (Copenhagen: Det Danske Selskab, 1983); and A. M. Allchin, D. Jasper, J. H. Schjørring, and K. Stevenson (eds), *Heritage and Prophecy: Grundtvig and the English-Speaking World* (Aarhus: University Press, 1993); there has been no specific study, so far as I know, of Grundtvig on the Transfiguration.

16. N. F. S. Grundtvig, *Christelige Prædikener eller Søndags-Bog I* (Kjøbenhavn: Wahl, 1827), pp. 1–18; Christian Thodberg (ed.), *Grundtvigs Prædikener* Vol. X (København: Gad, 1986), pp. 368–73; and Thodberg, *Grundtvigs Prædikener I Vartov* Vol. VI (København: Gad, 2006).

17. See texts in *Grundvigs Sangværk* Vols I, IV, V (København: Det Danske Forlag, 1944, 1949, 1951); Vol. I, No. 141 (pp. 316–20); Vol. IV, No. 250 (pp. 323–4), Nos. 371–2 (pp. 466–8); Vol. V, No. 223 (pp. 372–4).

18. Quoted by Allchin, *Grundtvig*, p. 161.

19. Allchin, *Grundtvig*, p. 309.

20. See text in *Celebrating Common Prayer: A Version of the Daily Office SSF* (London: Mowbray, 2002), p. 188.

CHAPTER 5: VISITORS

1. John Chrysostom, *Hom. in Matt.* 56.3 in *Nicene and Post-Nicene Fathers*, First Series, Vol. X, p. 346.

2. Andreopoulos, *Metamorphosis*, pp.244–9; for earlier icons, see pp. 83–100.

3. Andreopoulos, *Metamorphosis*, p. 227.

4. See colour reproductions in Andreopoulos, *Metamorphosis*, between pp. 160 and 161.

5. William Pringle (tr.), *John Calvin: Commentary on a Harmony of the Evangelists* Vol. II (Edinburgh: Calvin Translation Society, 1845), p. 311.

6. Swete, *The Gospel According to St Mark*, p. 188.

7. Heil, *The Transfiguration of Jesus*, p. 157; Lee, *Transfiguration*, p. 17; see also Heil's discussion of Moses and Elijah, pp. 95–113.
8. Origen, *Commentary on Matthew* XII.38; see Ch. 9 n. 13.
9. Calvin, *Harmony*, p. 311.
10. Lee, *Transfiguration*, p. 18.
11. Alfred Plummer, *The Gospel According to S. Luke*, International Critical Commentary Series (Edinburgh: T&T Clark, 1908), p. 251.
12. See J. N. D. Kelly, *Golden Mouth: The Story of John Chrysostom, Ascetic, Preacher, Bishop* (London: Duckworth, 1995).
13. Kelly, *Golden Mouth*, p. 90.
14. See text in *Nicene and Post-Nicene Fathers*, Second Series, Vol. X, pp. 345–51.
15. See Maurice Sachot, 'Le réemploi de l'homélie 56 *In Matthaeum* de Jean Chrysostome (BHGa 1984) dans deux homélies Byzantines sur la Transfiguration (BHG 1980k et a1985)', *Recherches des Sciences Religieuse* 57 (1983), pp. 123–46; see also his *Les Homélies Grecques sur la Transfiguration: Tradition manuscrite* (Paris: Centre National de la Recherche Scientifique, 1987).
16. John of Damascus, *Oratio in Transfigurationem* 9 in Migne, *Patrologia Graeca* 96.559–60; ET in McGuckin, *The Transfiguration of Christ in Scripture and Tradition*, pp. 214–15; Theophanes Ceramaeus (= Philagathos of Cerami), *Homilia* 59 in *Patrologia Graeca* 132.1027–8.
17. Basil of Seleucia, *Oratio* 40.2 in Migne, *Patrologia Graeca* 85.457–8.
18. See *Horae Semiticae V: The Commentaries of Ishod'ad of Merv* (Cambridge: University Press, 1911), pp. 67–8.
19. See J. S. Assemani, *Sancti Patris Ephraem Nostri Syri Opera Omnia* Vol. 2 (Rome: Vatican, 1732), pp. 41–9; ET with notes by Ephrem Lash, on website; on the authorship, see Sachot, *L'homélie pseudochrysostomienne sur la Transfiguration*, p. 442.
20. See *Grundtvigs Sangværk* I, p. 316 (No. 141), where all three are printed in italics; the word for 'manifest' in ordinary speech means 'obvious', but is made up of two words apposite for the context, 'soleklar', 'clear as the sun'; cf. *Grundtvigs Sangværk* IV, pp. 323–4 (No. 251), where he refers to them as 'friends from God's dwelling'; pp. 466–7 (No. 371), where he refers to Moses' burial but Elijah's ascension; pp. 467–8 (No. 372), where he contrasts Jesus' destiny with theirs; and V, pp. 372–4 (No. 223), where a similar point is made, when the opening line has only Jesus in italics, and 'only Jesus is the Messiah' in the third line.
21. See *The Christian Year: Collects and Post Communion Prayers for Sundays and Festivals* (London: Church House Publishing, 1997), p. 76; see p. 252, where its source is indicated, the corresponding Sunday provision in *The Alternative Service Book 1980*.

CHAPTER 6: ENTHUSIASM

1. *The Sermons of Mark Frank*, Library of Anglo-Catholic Theology (Oxford: Parker, 1849), p. 326 (*Sermon XLVII*).

2. See Dietrich Bonhoeffer, *Ethics* (London: Collins, Fontana Library, 1953).

3. Thomas Aquinas, *Summa Theologica* II/II.lxxvi.6, and *Sententiae* IV.xliv.2, quoted from Darwell Stone, *A History of the Doctrine of the Holy Eucharist* (Vol. I) (London: Longmans, 1909), p. 331, nn. 9 and 10.

4. A. M. Ramsey, *The Gospel and the Catholic Church* (London: Longmans, 1936), p. 111.

5. See Lee, *Transfiguration*, pp. 19–20 (Mark), 49–50 (Matthew), 75–6 (Luke); and Heil, *The Transfiguration of Jesus*, pp. 115–127; cf. Riesenfeld, *Jésu Transfiguré*, pp. 145–205.

6. Hacket, *A Century of Sermons*, p. 452 (from Sermon 5, entirely devoted to the Peter's suggestion, Luke 9:33).

7. See Heil, *The Transfiguration of Jesus*, pp. 158–63 (Mark), pp. 207–10 (Matthew), pp. 264–6 (Luke).

8. See Lee, *Transfiguration*, p. 50.

9. Basil of Seleucia, *Oratio* 40.3 in Migne, *Patrologia Graeca* 85.459–60; John of Damascus, *Monitum in Homiliam de Transfiguratione Domini* 16 in Migne, *Patrologia Graeca* 96.569–70; ET in McGuckin, *The Transfiguration of Christ in Scripture and Tradition*, pp. 220–2.

10. Augustine, *Sermon* 78.6, in Hill (tr.), *The Works of St Augustine: Sermons III/3*, p. 342.

11. See *Sermons on Important Subjects by the Revd. George Whitefield, with a Memoir on the author by Samuel Drew* (London: Tegg and Son, 1836), p. 346 (Sermon 30).

12. See article on Frank by Kenneth Stevenson in *The New Dictionary of National Biography*.

13. For John Cosin on the Transfiguration, see Kenneth Stevenson, 'The Liturgical Work of John Cosin: Some Remarks on Method' in Margot Johnson (ed.), *John Cosin: From Priest to Prince Bishop: Essays in Commemoration of the 400th Annniversary of his Birth* (Durham: Turnstone Ventures, 1997), pp. 214, 217 (whole essay, pp. 206–27); see also *The Works of John Cosin* Vol. V, Library of Anglo-Catholic Theology (Oxford: Parker, 1855), pp. 34–5 ('Particulars: First Series'); and G. J. Cuming, *The Durham Book* (London: Oxford University Press, 1961), p. 217. There are, perhaps surprisingly, practically no allusions to the Transfiguration in the sermons of Lancelot Andrewes.

14. For full text of sermon, see *The Sermons of Mark Frank* Vol. II, pp. 318–35: I hope that including Mark Frank here, justified in itself, also

makes up for his omission (my fault!) from the relevant part of Geoffrey Rowell, Kenneth Stevenson, and Rowan Williams (eds), *Love's Redeeming Work: The Anglican Quest for Holiness* (Oxford: University Press, 2001).

15. See below, Ch. 7 n. 5.
16. See Maurice Frost (ed.), *Historical Companion to Hymns Ancient and Modern* (London: Clowes, 1962), pp. 428–9 (Hymn 560).
17. John Inge, *A Christian Theology of Place*, Explorations in Practical, Pastoral and Empirical Theology (Aldershot: Ashgate, 2003), pp. 89–90.

CHAPTER 7: CLOUD

1. Gregory Palamas, *Homilia* 34 in Migne, *Patrologia Graeca* 151.431–2; ET in McGuckin, *The Transfiguration of Christ in Scripture and Tradition*, p. 230.
2. E.g. Lee, *Transfiguration*, p. 22: 'The cloud itself is not a natural phenomenon, any more than the light.'
3. Andrew Louth, 'From Doctrine of Christ to Icon of Christ: St Maximos the Confessor on the Transfiguration of Christ', forthcoming in the Brian Daley *Festschrift*.
4. See Maximus, *Chapters on Knowledge* II.16 in George C. Berthold (tr. and nn.), *Maximus Confessor: Selected Writings*, Classics of Western Spirituality (New York: Paulist Press, 1985), p. 151.
5. See R. Heber and C. P. Eden (eds), *The Works of Jeremy Taylor* Vol. II (London: Longmans, 1864), pp. 554–5 (= *The Great Exemplar* Pt. III Sec. XIII, Discourse on 'The Certainty of Salvation'); see also Henry McAdoo, *First of Its Kind: Jeremy Taylor's Life of Christ – A Study in the Functioning of a Moral Theology* (Norwich: Canterbury Press, 1994).
6. See Augustine Baker and Justin McCann (eds), *The Cloud of Unknowing* (London: Burns Oates, 1924), Ch. 75, pp. 98–9.
7. Evans, *Saint Luke*, p. 419.
8. See Heil, *The Transfiguration of Jesus*, pp. 129–49; cf. Riesenfeld, *Jésu Transfiguré*, pp. 130–45.
9. See Heil, *The Transfiguration of Jesus*, p. 131 n. 7, where he cites G. Lohfink, *Die Himmelfahrt Jesu; Untersuhungen zu den Himmelfahrtsund Erhöhungstexten bei Lukas*, Studien zum Alten und Neuen Testament 26 (Munich: Kösel, 1971), p. 191.
10. Timothy of Jerusalem, *In Crucem et in Transfigurationem*, and Euthymius Zigabenus, *Commentarium in Lucam* 30; texts in Migne, *Patrologia Graeca* 86.263–64; 129.949–50.
11. See Lee, *Transfiguration*, pp. 76–7: 'On balance, it is more likely that all six entered the cloud' (p. 76); Plummer veers towards restriction, *St Luke*, pp. 252–3.

12. Lee, *Transfiguration*, p. 22.

13. Lee, *Transfiguration*, p. 23.

14. See John Meyendorff, *A Study of Gregory Palamas* (London: Faith Press, 1964), quotation, p. 218; see also Norman Russell, *The Doctrine of Deification in the Greek Patristic Tradition*, Oxford Early Christian Studies (Oxford: Oxford University Press, 2004), pp. 304–9.

15. For the full texts of the homilies, see Migne, *Patrologia Graeca* 151.423–36 (*Homily* 34) and 435–50 (*Homily* 35): ET of *Homily* 34 in McGuckin, *The Transfiguration of Christ in Scripture and Tradition*, pp. 225–34, with extracts of *Homily* 35 on pp. 234–5. For the homily of Gregory the Sinaite, see David Balfour, 'Saint Gregory the Sinaite: Discourse on the Transfiguration', *Theologia* 52.4–54, 1 (1981/83), Athens, 1983, pp. 631–81.

16. John of Damascus, *Homilia in Transfiguratione* 10 in Migne, *Patrologia Graeca* 96.561–2; ET in McGuckin, *The Transfiguration of Christ in Scripture and Tradition*, p. 215.

17. McGuckin, *The Transfiguration of Christ in Scripture and Tradition*, p. 119.

18. See Andrew of Crete, *Oratio* 7 in Migne, *Patrologia Graeca* 97.933–4, where he refers to the day as a 'feast of deification'; cf. Theophanes Cermaeus (= Philagathos of Cerami), '*tetheōmenon sōma*' ('body made into God'), of Christ on the mountain, *Homilia* LIX in *Patrologia Graeca* 132.1033–4.

19. Evelyn Underhill, *The Light of Christ* (London: Longmans, 1944), pp. 45f.

CHAPTER 8: VOICE

1. Peter the Venerable, *Sermon* I in Migne, *Patrologia Latina* 189.970.

2. Andreopoulos, *Metamorphosis*, pp. 83–100: see Ch. 5 n. 2.

3. See Kenneth W. Stevenson, *The Lord's Prayer: A Text in Tradition* (London: SCM Press/Minneapolis: Fortress Press, 2004), pp. 220–34.

4. Heil, *The Transfiguration of Jesus*, pp. 163–70 (Mark), pp. 210–19 (Matthew), pp. 268–76 (Luke).

5. Lee, *Transfiguration*, p. 24.

6. See Bede, *In Matthaei Evangelium Expositio* III in Migne, *Patrologia Latina* 92.81.

7. Lee, *Transfiguration*, pp. 57–8.

8. Schweizer, *The Good News According to Mark*, p. 183.

9. Rabanus Maurus, *Commentarium in Matthaeum* V.17; Ralph of Laon, *Glossa Ordinaria in Matthaeum* XVII; Peter of Celle, *Sermon* 65; texts in Migne, *Patrologia Latina* 107.1000; 114.144; 202.843. Andrew of Crete, *Oratio* 7; Timothy of Jerusalem, *In Crucem et in Transfigurationem*; texts in Migne, *Patrologia Graeca* 97.953–954; 86.263–264.

10. For the sermon, see Peter the Venerable, *Sermon* 1 in Migne, *Patrologia Latina* 189.953–72; see also Jean Leclercq, *Pierre le Vénérable* (Abbaye S. Wandrille: Éditions de Fontenelle, 1946), pp. 325–31 (discussion of the sermon), pp. 379–89 (discussion of the Office, followed by the texts); and Pfaff, *New Liturgical Feasts in Later Medieval England*, pp. 13–39.

11. See Leclercq, *Pierre le Vénérable*, p. 385.

12. On Jerome, see Ch. 2 n. 14.

13. On Chrysostom, see Ch. 5 n. 14.

14. See G. G. Willis, 'The Offertory Prayers and the Canon' in *Essays in Early Roman Liturgy*, Alcuin Club Collections 46 (London: SPCK, 1964), p. 109.

15. See Frost (ed.), *Historical Companion to Hymns Ancient and Modern*, p. 318 (No. 331).

16. Peter Shaw, *Conversation Matters: How to Engage Effectively with One Another* (London: Continuum, 2004), pp. 178–9. I am indebted to Kitty Price for much assistance here.

CHAPTER 9: DESCENT

1. Origen, *Contra Celsum* 2.64 in *The Ante-Nicene Fathers* Vol. IV (Edinburgh: T&T Clark, 1994), p. 457; the translation here is from an extract in McGuckin, *The Transfiguration of Christ in Scripture and Tradition*, p. 151.

2. See Ch. 7 n. 7.

3. Rowan Williams, *Ponder These Things* (Norwich: Canterbury Press, 2002), p. xi.

4. See Heil, *The Transfiguration of Jesus*, pp. 174–5 (Mark), pp. 223–5 (Matthew), pp. 275–6 (Luke).

5. See Lee, *Transfiguration*, pp. 23, 25.

6. See Lee, *Transfiguration*, p. 59.

7. See Lee, *Transfiguration*, p. 81.

8. Raymond E. Brown, *The Death of the Messiah* Vol. 1 (London: Chapman, 1994), p. 291.

9. John Chrysostom, *Homilies on John* 88.1 in *The Nicene and Post-Nicene Fathers*, First Series, Vol. XIV (Edinburgh: T&T Clark, 1996), p. 331.

10. John McGuckin (ed.), *The Westminster Handbook to Origen*, Westminster Handbooks to Christian Theology (Louisville KY: Westminster John Knox Press, 2004), p. 30.

11. Origen, *Commentary on Matthew* XII.29–43 in *The Ante-Nicene Fathers* Vol. X (Edinburgh: T&T Clark, 1995), pp. 465–73; see the Greek text, Erich Klostermann (ed.), *Origenes Werke: Zehnter Band: Origenes Matthäuserklärung: I* (Leipzig: Hinrich, 1935), pp. 148–70. See also

Louth's remarks on Origen in 'St Augustine's Interpretation of the Transfiguration of Christ', pp. 375–7; and also Kenneth Stevenson, 'From Origen to Palamas: Greek expositions of the Transfiguration', a paper read at the Society for Oriental Liturgy, Eichstätt, July 2006.

12. Tertullian, *Adversus Marcionem* 4.22 in *The Ante-Nicene Fathers* Vol. III (Edinburgh: T&T Clark, 1993), p. 383.
13. Origen, *Commentary on Matthew* XII.17 in *The Ante-Nicene Fathers* Vol. X, p. 460.
14. See Origen, *On Prayer* 26.2 in John O'Meara (ed. and tr.), *Origen: Prayer, Exhortation to Martyrdom*, Ancient Christian Writers 19 (New York: Newman Press, 1934), p. 88; see also Stevenson, *The Lord's Prayer*, p. 14 (Origen), p. 52 (Ps-Chrysostom, 'Opus Imperfectum'), p. 129 (Meister Eckhart), p. 169 (Catechism of the Council of Trent, early editions only), p. 223 (Westcott and Hort).
15. Ephrem, *Commentary on Diatessaron* XIV.10 in Leloir (ed.), *Éphrem de Nisibe: Commentaire sur l'Évangile concordant ou Diatessaron*, p. 248.
16. Gottfried of Admont, *Homily* 28 in Migne, *Patrologia Latina* 174.191.
17. Alexandra Stevenson drew my attention to this. See Fabrizio Mancinelli, *A Masterpiece Close-Up: The Transfiguration by Raphael* (Vatican: Museums and Galleries, 1977).
18. *Book of Lutheran Worship* (Minneapolis: Augsburg Publishing House, 1978), pp. 137, 153.

CHAPTER 10: DISCIPLESHIP TRANSFIGURED

1. Lee, *Transfiguration*, pp. 124–5.
2. Cf. the Armenian tradition of observing the feast on the fiftieth day after Pentecost, the hundredth day after Easter; I am indebted to George Leylegian for assistance here.
3. McGuckin's *The Transfiguration of Christ in Scripture and Tradition* (pp. 129–322) is the nearest we have to such a collection, but it needs to be fuller.
4. Ramsey, *The Glory of God and the Transfiguration of Christ*, p. 145.
5. See Kenneth Stevenson, '"Rooted in Detachment": Transfiguration as Narrative, Worship and Community of Faith' in *Ecclesiology* 1.3 (2005), pp. 22–6 (whole article, pp. 13–26).
6. F. D. Maurice, *The Gospel of the Kingdom: A Course of Lectures upon the Gospel of St Luke* (London: Macmillan, 1864), p. 152.
7. Kenneth Leech, 'Transfiguration and Disfiguration', *Fairacres Chronicle* 38.2 (2005), p. 8 (whole sermon pp. 5–9): I am indebted to John Pinder for drawing my attention to this.
8. See Luz, *Matthew 8—20: A Commentary*, p. 394.
9. See in general Lee, *Transfiguration*, p. 92.
10. See Dorothy Lee's observations about the three disciples as men,

and the place of women in the Fourth Gospel, where there is no Transfiguration narrative, *Transfiguration*, pp. 130–1.

11. See Rowan Williams, *Grace and Necessity: Reflections on Art and Love* (London: Morehouse, 2005), p. 163.

12. See the themes discussed by McGuckin, *The Transfiguration of Christ in Scripture and Tradition*, pp. 99–128; cf. the comparable list in Luz's treatment, *Matthew 8—20: A Commentary*, pp. 393–414.

13. Lewis Wolpert, *Six Impossible Things Before Breakfast: The Evolutionary Origins of Belief* (London: Faber and Faber, 2006), p. 220.

14. See J. K. Rowling, *Harry Potter and the Philosopher's Stone* (London: Bloomsbury, 1997), p. 100.

15. See Mother Mary and Archimandrite Kallistos Ware (tr.), *The Festal Menaion* (London: Faber and Faber, 1969), p. 470; Greek text in Cosmas of Jerusalem, *Hymns* XI in Migne, *Patrologia Graeca* 98.521–2.

16. See Frost (ed.), *Historical Companion to Hymns Ancient and Modern*, p. 130 (Hymn 7); it first appeared in one of the earliest collections of hymns, the 1740 edition of *Hymns and Spiritual Poems*; see also J. Ernest Rattenbury, *The Evangelical Doctrine of Charles Wesley's Hymns* (London: Epworth, 1941), p. 348 (cf. p. 164 on the Christology of this hymn).

INDEX

Steiner, George 50, 163 n.2
Stephen, St 56, 61, 162 n.5
Swete, H.B. 19, 160 n.4

Tatian 21
Taylor, Jeremy 92, 101, 167 n.5
Tertullian 3, 140, 170 n.12
Theophanes the Greek viii, 2, 30,
    36, 67, 82, 94, 102, 115, 131,
    133, 153
Thomas Aquinas 84, 166 n.3

Thorvaldsen, Bertel 62
Timothy of Jerusalem 7, 103, 122,
    159 n.14, 167 n.10, 168 n.9

Underhill, Evelyn 112, 168 n.19

Wesley, Charles 156, 171 n.16
Whitefield, George 90, 166 n.11
Williams, Rowan ix, 133, 153, 167
    n.14, 169 n.3, 171 n.11
Wolpert, Lewis 154, 171 n.13